EX LIBRIS
DOLORES WRIGHT

REPORT TO
SAINT PETER

upon the kind of world in which
Hendrik Willem van Loon
spent the first years
of his life

Written and illustrated by
Hendrik Willem van Loon

NEW YORK · 1947
SIMON AND SCHUSTER

TO JIMMIE

I cannot keep a record of my life by my actions. Fortune placed them too low. I can, however, keep it by my thoughts.

MONTAIGNE

INTRODUCTION

HENDRIK WILLEM VAN LOON'S *last book,* Report to Saint Peter, *is a fragment. It came to his publishers, some weeks after his death—a manuscript of less than two hundred pages, written on that substantial orange-yellow paper on which so many of his famous books were composed. As the editor with whom Hendrik Willem had worked for many years, I was elected to make the first examination of the pathetically light package (his solo performances were usually bulky, products of a full mind and a generous heart). Intended as an* Apologia pro vita sua *(for what else should a report to Saint Peter be?), it scarcely takes Hendrik Willem into his grammar-school days. The autobiographer, allowing the reader a few enchanting squints at the peepshow of his childhood, at almost all times defers to the humanist. The result is a series of those free historical fantasias with which Hendrik Willem delighted millions of readers, the world over, for more than a quarter of a century.*

During the last few months of his life, when Hendrik Willem was giving what was left of him to the war effort and related activities (work enough to strain the vitality of a thoroughly healthy man), I lost track of the sequence of book ideas that, in those last days, could be pursued only in "spare time." Therefore, I realized that Mrs. van Loon alone could tell Hendrik Willem's readers how Report to Saint Peter, *with its prophetic title, came to be written. At first it was my intention to abstract whatever data she gave me; but when this letter came from Old Greenwich, I concluded that it would be an impertinence to do anything else than reproduce it in full.*

WALLACE BROCKWAY

Introduction

January 8, 1946

DEAR WALLACE:

You have asked me how Hendrik Willem came to write Report to Saint Peter. *Well, it was like this.*

Another major book was about due. The last one had been Van Loon's Lives. *After that, a couple of music books with Grace Castagnetta and a couple of short biographies—Thomas Jefferson and Simón Bolivar.* Lives *had been published in 1942, and it was already 1943. Another "big book" was definitely indicated.*

For a dozen years or more, Hendrik had been fascinated by the title The Average Man, *but he never could find an approach to the thing. When you get right down to cases, an average man does merely average things, and there is not much dramatic appeal—nothing to hang a* major opus *around. One might as well read the stories in* The Ladies' Home Journal. *The trials and tribulations of a soap-opera heroine are, thank God, beyond the average calamities which hit mankind.*

Many people had been suggesting that Hendrik write his autobiography, and I wanted him very much to do it. He had been around—even around the world on a nice, safe, conducted tour—but he always saw many things that the average eye missed. But Han was very shy about it. Finally he said that if I thought it a good idea, he would go ahead "but there will be no bios *in it." (He was rather pleased with his Dutch schoolboy knowledge of Greek. In his day, the poor little devils all had to take it.) So sometime during the summer of 1943 he started in. He began on the pictures. He always did. He liked to draw much more than he liked to write. Unfortunately, the books always made much more money than the pictures.*

Well, the autobiography went along for a short space of time, and then suddenly he hit on a title which intrigued him —Report to Saint Peter. He said it would make things easier

*for the old saint when he rapped for admittance at the pearly
gates if he had it all written down in advance for him.*

I was personally convinced after the first few pages that the
Report *was going to be* the *book, and Hendrik liked it himself, and everybody who came to call had to read the manuscript as far as he had it. My Line-a-Day Book gives a date:
Sept. 24, 1943. "M.H. called in morning to read* St. Peter."

Early in December, Hendrik was asked to write an Army
Guide to Holland, *in line with all the other little guidebooks
that the army was then publishing (he never finished it, by the
way), and that threw him off the* Report *for the time being.
He decided to write a new history of the world instead.*

*On January 8, 1944, my Line-a-Day Book reports as follows:
"Han decided to drop the new history and do* The Average
Man *instead." He dropped that after having written a short
foreword and began* The Life and Times of Gustavus Vasa,
*to be included in the series of juvenile biographies, along with
Jefferson and Bolívar. (Vasa was published in the summer of
1945 by Dodd, Mead.)*

*February of 1944 was a bad month. One heart attack after
another. The war was going badly, and he was terribly worried
about that. Ideas for one book after another passed through
his tired mind. On the night of March 10, he decided to write
a history of the eighteenth century, and went happily to bed
full of his new program. The next morning he died.*

*And this, Wallace, is about all I can tell you about the be-
ginning of* Report to Saint Peter. *He would return to it from
time to time between interruptions, but he was too tired and
too sick to keep at it for any length of time. I hope this gives
you what you need.*

JIMMIE

TABLE OF CONTENTS

xi

Table of Contents

ILLUSTRATIONS

Illustrations

PROLOGUE AROUND THE GATE OF HEAVEN

IT WAS Sunday evening, and we were having supper on the front porch, for it was a warm day early in June, and we were happy that at last we had been able to eat out in the open. Suzanne and Joep Nicolas had brought a friend—a Dutchman and a Franciscan. Dutchmen are no novelty in my life, but, like all good Hollanders brought up in an atmosphere of the old-fashioned liberalism, I had met very few Franciscans. The only type of clerics with whom I had ever been in personal contact had been Jesuits, and I had not taken to them any too kindly, as they were forever trying to convert me, a form of spiritual activity I have always greatly resented, no matter from what side it comes. Therefore, when Suzanne and Joep appeared with their man of God, I whispered to Jimmie, "Lord help us all!" and she quickly replied, "Hold your horses. It may not be as bad as you think."

And it was not. I did not even have to hold my horses. I could let them trot and gallop and scamper to my heart's delight. I could even harness them as I pleased, troika fashion or tandem, it made no difference. For the good father was a joy to any civilized human being. Of course, I might have known as much, since the Nicolases had brought him; for Joep is a Limburger (a type of citizen highly superior to one born in the austere climate of the Calvinist-ridden province of Holland) and knows his priests as my son of the Vermont orchards knows his apples.

The evening therefore developed into a feast of general good will, and the lion and the lamb gamboled together as happily and as unconcernedly as if they had been lifelong friends, which they undoubtedly became that very evening. When I had a chance to get Joep alone for a moment, I said, "Where in heaven's name did you find him? A Jesuit who makes himself agreeable to everybody he meets!"

"Jesuit!" Joep answered. "My dear Hendrik, I would never do that to you. No, this fellow is a Franciscan, and you will love him." As indeed I came to do, only regretting that I made such bad material as a possible convert, for I can go just so far in my dealings with any kind of creed.

Of course, since each of us loves an argument, we fought tooth and nail, but our spiritual and intellectual wrestling match resembled those curious gladiatorial combats in which Mungo, our Newfoundland dog, and our kitten used to indulge in the days of their youth. One should have seen them (as many people did) to appreciate what I mean by this reference. Occasionally the kitten would disappear entirely in Mungo's vast jaw with its rows of wolflike fangs. The next moment the kitten would jump straight into the air and land on Mungo's back with its hair standing on end and all of its twenty claws ready to grip and tear. But no harm was ever done. The teeth never bit and the claws never scratched, for they were dearly devoted to each other and were only having fun.

And so that evening became a happy milestone along the road of friendship (now so heavily damaged by the bombs and shells of that unspeakable little postcard artist of the Wilhelmstrasse) and, God willing (concession to the beloved Suzanne's way of feeling about such things), it will lead to a great many others, planted in the uncertain landscape of the future.

As was to have been expected, on some minor points we failed to see eye to eye. But what matter such trivial details as long as two people agree upon the basic essentials of life, such as kindliness, charity, forbearance, and good will towards all men and women of good will? And we were very careful to respect each other's views upon that one point which, these last two thousand years, has been responsible for such infinite misery and for the shedding of so much innocent blood. One of us "believed," and the other confessed that the wonder of creation was beyond him and that therefore he must let it go at a mere "I don't know, and, since I shall never know, I merely accept and ask no questions."

This answer somewhat nettled the good father. "But you must feel the need of some kind of guidance in your life?" he objected. "You surely do not claim that you can get everything out of your own inner consciousness?"

"Of course not," I told him, "but what more do I need than the companionship of Socrates and Spinoza and Kant, with incidental music by Bach and Mozart?"

He did not then answer me, but a few days later he sent me a little story. As it is done in the best Franciscan style, I shall here give it to you in a translation which tries very hard to reveal the delicate intonations of the original Dutch. It is called *Hendrik Willem Goes to Heaven* and reads as follows:

It had not been easy but at last it had been successfully accomplished, and Hendrik Willem's soul had set itself free from the ponderous body which had been its terrestrial home. During so many years had it been an intimate part of the millions of cells which composed this vast substance (Hendrik Willem had been created along rather Gargantuan lines) that it had become thoroughly attached to its abode. But now at last the time had come for the two to bid each other farewell, and the soul had escaped.

"Brother Ass, the body," remained behind—alone. A great many people came to look at him, and on his final little excursion he was accompanied by a large number of people, for both high and low wanted to pay honor to his memory. Many a solemn word was spoken before he was committed to the earth, but on this occasion (very much contrary to his habit) Hendrik Willem did not indulge in any back talk. He kept as quiet as one had reason to expect of a person in his condition and, to tell you the truth, he no longer cared. For him the case had been settled for good and all.

Neither did he bother greatly that no one appeared to accompany his soul. He liked a little loneliness after always having been surrounded by so many people; furthermore, it did not last long, for almost immediately he reached a fork of the road where, of all people, he came upon Dante. The distinguished Florentine informed him that one of those two roads led upward, while the other led downward—a fact that was no news to Hendrik Willem. He had known that ever since he was a little boy. But, as he had never liked going downward, he felt little desire to follow that dismal track. Then he discovered that there was still a third way, a narrow path that seemed to be some kind of detour; but he thought it would be a waste of time to follow that, and so, without any further hesitation, he continued on his way—upward, of course.

When he reached the end he noticed that Saint John had been quite correct in the description he had given of the place in his well-known volume of Revelation. Quite naturally, Hendrik Willem felt that he should make straight for the main entrance. After all, the Good Lord could only be happy that so famous a writer and speaker had arrived to add a little gaiety to the life of this settlement, which undoubtedly was a happy one but which at the same time might have a tendency towards the monotony implicit in the idea of eternity. But some slight feeling of doubt prevented him from going ahead too fast. The keeper of the gate was surely no Cerberus, seeing that he had been the first of the Popes, but at the same time there was always the possibility that this venerable old gentleman might raise some objection to letting someone who had never belonged to the flock have direct access to the Shepherd Himself. Hendrik Willem wisely decided to go and see whether he could not find some less pretentious back door, and behold! just as he had expected, in his subconscious mind, he found one.

It was a small ivy-clad gate, and in front of it stood Saint Francis. A pigeon was perched on the top of his hood, and a couple of little rabbits were playing at his feet. Of course, the first thing good Francis did was to invite this stranger to come in. A curiously assorted group of people were assembled in the rose garden of the minstrel of the Lord. There were artists and idealists, troubadours and many animals of the field, adventurers, fiddlers, mystics, poets, and players on the harpsichord—some looking very respectable and others not quite so respectable. In one corner, Saint Solanus * stood all by himself, busily engaged with his violin. In another part of the garden, Christopher Columbus was engaged in an animated conversation about telescopes. His partner was that experienced lens specialist, Baruch de Spinoza, and Hendrik Willem observed that this friendly-looking little Jew seemed to feel much more at home in a sunny garden than in those whitewashed chambers, Calvinistically austere, in which he had been obliged to spend most of his days. And of course Dante was there too, for in spite of everything he seemed to prefer the Poverello's "Hymn to the Sun" to the *Summa* of Thomas of Aquinas. He also noticed Ruysbroeck, the Flemish mystic, who was whiling away the time of day with Louis Pasteur. Vittoria Colonna and Margherita of Cortona were also present, but now, with great and becoming modesty, they were sitting at the feet of Dame Poverty.

Right opposite this little garden, on the other side of the street, stood the College of Saint Ignatius. The very outside betrayed an air of severity: instinctively, you felt that within its heavy walls the atmosphere must be quite different from the spirit of gaiety which prevailed among the rose shrubs of Saint Francis, and that the inhabitants of the premises formed by no means so heterogeneous a group as those who had gathered together to partake of the Franciscan sunshine. The spiritual exercises of Don Ignacio

---

* This holy personage, like Saint Niobe in *Ivanhoe,* is unknown to hagiology. Apparently, the author generated him from *sol* and *la.*—Ed.

had done their work. All the inmates had been formed after a single pattern, and Hendrik Willem thanked his stars that his feet had not carried him to the wrong gate. For he felt himself thoroughly at home among his new friends. No sooner had Spinoza seen him than he rushed forward with a happy smile of recognition and at once told him that their host, Saint Francis, had been much wiser than all these other and most learned people who were walking around him.

"And that goes for me too," he said, "for I had better make this clear. Otherwise, since you have so recently left our pedantic Dutch brethren, you might suspect that I think more of my work than I do."

In this way the ice was broken, and Hendrik Willem felt completely at home. Soon the conversation became general, and Hendrik Willem naturally took his share.

And then—suddenly—there was a great silence. Everybody ceased to speak except the birds, who sang even more beautifully than before. Surrounded by angels playing the lute, the Lord appeared, as He did every day at this hour, taking His afternoon walk through the little garden of Saint Francis. He stopped for a moment and in a friendly sort of way let His eyes dwell upon the company until He noticed the new guest. Then, slightly turning, He beckoned to Saint Francis and asked who the stranger might be.

Well, at first Saint Francis did not quite know what to say and looked a little embarrassed, but after a moment's hesitation he answered, "He is quite all right, dear Lord. He is really very nice. You see, he invited me to dinner once in Veere—in that old Dutch village where he lived before the war—and so, of course, what else could I do but welcome him? And he has always been very good to the poor—he really has shared his wealth with anyone who needed it—and You know what Your Son said upon that subject, so I thought it would be . . ." But he did not have to continue, for the Lord made a gesture which meant, "That will do. I know what you mean," and He smiled quietly at Saint Francis and went His way.

Hendrik Willem saw that smile, and it made him very happy —happier indeed than he had ever been, for now he knew that the

kindness of the Lord is still greater—yes, infinitely greater—than
that of good Saint Francis.

That was the story the good father had sent me, and I must
confess that I liked it. Of course I was flattered by the compliment he paid me in making me the center of his little dis-
course. But the tale had an undoubted quality of Franciscan
charm, and I would have been delighted with it, no matter
who had been chosen to act as its hero. So I put it on my desk
that I might translate it for the benefit of those members of my
family who are not familiar with our ancestral language, and
then there were many annoying little jobs that had to be done,
and so it became one of those things which we must do tomorrow, but then absolutely and no mistake about it—it must
be done!

Then, however, came that period in my life (known to all
authors) when I had successfully finished one job and must
look for a new one. The *Lives* had made their appearance, and
now what next? A great many people clamored for more Dutch
parties with the departed. "You can just as well entertain your
spooky guests in the Nieuw Veere as in the old one. We want
a lot more of that sort of entertainment, and next time please
write . . ." and then there followed a list of their favorite
historical characters, often augmented with suggestions for the
kind of repast I should prepare for them and the kind of music
they might like to hear.

This was very nice. It established that direct and personal
tie between the author and his readers for which all writers
hope and pray, but which few of them are ever able to establish.
But the idea was not practical. In the first place, "literary re-
peats" (unless they deal with orangutans or sweet-souled little
girls) are invariably disastrous to a writer's reputation. The
public resents them. "This fellow has hit a strain which he has
found to be profitable and now he is going to cash in on it,"

they invariably say. The readers resent being treated as a sort of milch cow, which from now on exists solely for the purpose of keeping its owner in a state of comfortable affluence. And as far as I am concerned, the reading public is right—quite right—in its suspicions.

And then there were certain other considerations of equal weight. The old Veere, with its thousand-year-old memories, was just the right spot for those curious little parties with which Frits (God bless his memory!) and I tried to amuse our queer collection of guests. They knew that they would enjoy absolute privacy, that their comings and goings would remain unnoticed, and that even if they were observed by some belated villager he would merely wish them a pleasant good evening but would not dream of asking them upon what kind of mission they were bound.

Lucas Point, let me hasten to add, is quite as careful in its observance of its neighbors' private concerns as the old Veere was. Indeed, that's one of the main reasons that I love the place and hope to be able to spend the rest of my days right there. Those who live around me accept me as I am, and if the endless hours I am forced to sit at my desk (fishing little words out of a ten-cent bottle of ink) prevent me from partaking of the communal life as frequently as I would like to do, they don't seem to resent it. They know that I hold them, their children, and their dogs in high esteem and affection, and they are satisfied to let me lead my own kind of life, as it has been imposed upon me by the necessity of making a living out of nothing more than books—for the magazines and the radio and the movies have a well-founded fear of anything I write or say. They are subject to the revenge of all the myriad pressure groups which make the country unsafe for a true democracy, and, since they are engaged in the business of making money and cannot afford to incur the displeasure of a single customer, they must forever be on their guard against the moronic blasts of even the dumbest of their listeners or readers. I therefore do not blame them if they most carefully avoid any personal contact with this unreconstructed liberal, for even if my text (blue-penciled by a dozen censors) seemed as innocuous as the platform of a political convention, I might, by certain intonations, reveal what is really on my mind and in my heart.

I therefore depend for my daily bread and butter (and an occasional box of candy for the grandchildren) on my books. Any author will tell you how difficult that is, and I have good reason to be grateful that for the last twenty years I have been able to do so. Of course, I have been most fortunate in my publishers. They have been both patient and understanding, and in all financial matters they have treated me like the idiot I happen to be when it comes to money and have undoubtedly saved me more than once from complete disaster.

But of all this I will, of course, speak in much greater detail later on. I mention it now only to make it clear that the choice of the subject of a new book means much more to me than merely a fresh title and a list of chapter headings. It may make the difference between eating and going hungry, and it is therefore a matter which deserves the most careful consideration.

Those *inter libros* periods are particularly hard on Jimmie, for she is obliged to listen to my groans and mumblings when at breakfast, lunch, and dinner I curse the profession I have chosen (as if ever I had had any other choice or would have willed it!); but she, as the only person capable of deciphering my manuscripts, is under the necessity of copying an endless number of forewords to an equally endless number of volumes, each one of which is "absolutely the right book for me to do next!" until a few hours later it is superseded by an even more "absolutely right" idea which has come to me after an afternoon nap. For we are early risers and late-to-bed goers and need an hour's snooze after lunch.

Generally speaking, I know very well in what general direction I should look for my next "offering," as they say at upstate musical entertainments. My sons and my correspondents have left no doubt about what was expected of me. If there is anything that has made me grateful for the craft I have chosen, it is the response to my work by the boys in the Army and Navy. In spite of all sorts of difficulties (and try and get a book not on officially "preferred lists" in Cairo or Reykjavik, unless you know Egyptian or Icelandic), they seem somehow to be able to get hold of my books, and their letters have made up for the endless hours of the hardest kind of labor that have gone into those hefty volumes. They write to me in that friendly spirit which always should exist (and sometimes actually does) between an intelligent student and a ditto professor. They often voice their doubts and ask questions, and they have to make suggestions which quite often set me thinking along lines that prove to be highly useful when I start work on something else. But there invariably comes a sort of general P.S.: "You have now told us all about the arts (or geography or history, as the case may be, and thanks for the compliment). Now will you please and in very simple words and pictures tell us what this world is all about? They gave us a job to do—they told us to get rid of Hitler and Mussolini and to show the Japs what is what and teach them never again to pull that sort of stunt on free Americans, and we will do the job assigned. But when peace comes back—and one day peace will come just as suddenly as the war did—then what? Does it mean going back to work for some bastard in an office (I am sorry, but that is the word most of them use), getting married and having a house in some suburb, raising a couple of kids, and struggling the rest of our lives to keep ahead of the insurance man and the fellow who holds the mortgage? Now, we are good Americans and we don't believe in any of the Bolshevik nonsense, though those fellows do know how to fight. But is everything to be just as it always was, and why is everything the way it is? You seem to be able to make complicated things simple; therefore please tell us what it is all about."

Such letters touch me deeply. The task entrusted to those lads (and many of them are so pathetically young—mere kids) is so terrific and so hideous that we owe them something more than the platitudes of the Four Freedoms or the vague promises of an Atlantic Charter. And I have spent forty years of my life reading and sometimes actually thinking, and all the time trying to find out—as well as I could—what it was that made people click. Some of my information about the mistakes of the past might be of help to these youngsters in avoiding at least a few of these errors in the future. But how and in what way could I tell them what they should know in a manner that would hold their interest and that would not be merely a repetition of the things I had already written down in so many of my other books?

The *Lives* was about the best approach I could think of, but the *Lives* was out of the question. It could not possibly be repeated. Then what? Then followed two miserable years of indecision and so many futile attempts that every time I offered still a new foreword for still a new book (this time "definitely the right one"), Jimmie, with her irrepressible habit of punning, would hail me with a sad "Oh, my God! Foreword march again, but how far will you go this time?" And she was right. I would do thirty or forty pages and then I would realize that once more I was barking up the wrong tree. Then these discarded bits of manuscript would go into the drawers of my desk until there were so many that I had to relegate them to the attic.

All of them bore queer titles: *The Mills of the Gods, The Garden of the God* (influence of my early taste for Anatole France), *The Average Man, The Great Event, Hannibal's Elephant* (God knows why, but at the moment I wrote that piece it seemed to make sense), *The Reporter at Large, Man.*

kind Revisited, I Was There, The Tower Talks, The New Perspective, The Old Perspective, and dozens of others of the same fantastic ilk, not to speak of a trilogy on the history of the Netherlands. If I had gone on that way much longer, both Jimmie and I would have gone completely crazy. I had to make a decision and then stick to it.

My choice, then, had narrowed down to two possibilities. One was an autobiography in which, while I would tell as little as possible about myself (after all, I have lived a very quiet sort of life—I have never even been a member of a town council), I would write about everything I had seen and heard and would offer my own commentaries as I went along. The other was a series of eight volumes, retelling, but in much greater detail, everything I had already written down in my *Story of Mankind.*

The latter idea struck me as best. Of course, at sixty-one one does not feel very happy at the prospect of a sixteen-year stretch at hard labor. One is not even sure of the day after tomorrow, what with a wobbly heart and the other inevitable ailments of advancing age. But just then I had come upon Theodor Lessing's *Geschichte als Sinngebung des Sinnlosen* and had been tremendously struck by his thesis that it was the duty of history to give meaning to that which otherwise would make no sense and to make sense of that which otherwise would have no meaning.

Until then I had always been vaguely under the influence of old Ranke's noble dictum that it was up to history to find out *wie es eigentlich dagewesen,* to discuss as carefully as possible what had happened and how it had actually come to pass. But here was an entirely new perspective. I remembered that Theodor Lessing, a very learned man, both a Ph.D. and an M.D., had been one of the most courageous opponents of the doctrines of Adolf Hitler, and I knew of course that the house painter's wrath had finally overtaken him and that he had been shot to death by a group of Nazi gangsters in Marienbad, Czechoslovakia, where he had found a refuge on his way to America. This I had read in the papers, and like most newspapermen I have the sort of brain which does not forget that kind of detail. I had also been told (I have forgotten by whom) that he had preached some sort of new idea about history, but what it was I had not known until I came upon a copy of his book.

It has happened a few times in my life that a sentence I casually found somewhere in a book changed my entire point of view with the suddenness of a revelation. To be sure, I have never experienced anything of the sort in the accepted religious sense of the word. History is full of such examples: Saint Paul, Luther, Pascal, to name only a few, were more fortunate than I. The sudden death of a friend, a thunderstorm, a mysterious voice from heaven changed their entire outlook upon life and turned them from sinners into saints. Maybe that is still awaiting me. But upon several occasions I know that some quite inconsequential sentence (which may have meant nothing in particular to the author) gave my own line of thinking a twist which led me into an entirely new field of speculation. And I owe it to the late Theodor Lessing that, when most of my work had already been done, I at last came upon that remark which made me see everything I had done so far as a sort of waste and which showed me the angle from which I should always have approached my historical writing.

The sad part was that it came to me so late in life. For I should need sixteen years in which to rewrite my history of the world, and I couldn't very well see myself at the age of seventy-six still two years away from scribbling *finis* on the last page of Volume VIII. I could of course (and I would—of that I was quite certain) let everything else I was ever to write be dominated by the magnificent idea that it was the purpose of history to give meaning to that which otherwise would make no sense. But eight volumes of seven hundred pages each, and sixteen years with no letup in a daily grind of ten hours: it was not a pleasant prospect. However, since it seemed a much better idea than the autobiography, I boldly set to work and wrote the first three chapters of my *Rise and Fall of the Age of Reason,* for I intended to begin with the eighteenth century, as the period I knew best of all.

And then my son Willem happened to drop in one fine morning with twenty-four-hour leave. During the afternoon, while he was getting ready to go back (what with belated trains and the lack of space, now that all our newly-rich war workers are traveling like mad), I mentioned my difficulties to him, but, as I had done this so often before and did not want to bore him (he was with me for so short a time anyhow), I said, "Oh, by the way, Son, have you ever read this little piece our Franciscan friend wrote for me?" For the folder which held the three pages was once more on my desk, and this time I was going to get down to the translation, if I never did anything else. Willem's Dutch is not too fluent, but he has a good musical ear (which is the same as having a gift for languages), and he could easily find his way through the original version, though it was composed in that tongue in which (as all the Dutch farmers of my childhood days firmly believed) the Lord had originally written the books of the Old Testament.

Willem picked it up. I threw him a cigarette, and he read while I went on with my interminable *History of the World* in eight volumes (will I still be able to hold a pen at seventy-seven or will I be like? . . . but never mind, it has got to be done). I had reached the chapter about Louis XIV and had had a very clever idea—so clever that I was quite proud of it. My King was dead to begin with. There was no doubt about that. The register of his demise was signed by the Cardinal Archbishop of Paris, by the keeper of the great seal, and by the head of the royal household. Old Louis was as dead as a doornail, and the court could go back to its regular business. "There," I said to myself, "that will hold them! Dickens' *Christmas Carol* mixed right into the text of a regular history, like the snatches of a popular tune which Gracie * used to play through the most ponderous parts of her concerts. The brighter members of the audience used to get it and were of course delighted and asked for more. The others did not. They would have been shocked if they had been told. It will be the same with my history. But this time I am going to write as I please. And I will do it again. There is a passage in *Henry Esmond* . . . but who reads *Henry Esmond* nowadays?"

That reminded me that on his last leave I had given Willem a copy of that book which when I first got hold of it (I must have been seventeen or eighteen) fascinated me so much that it made me learn English. Without *Henry Esmond* (even if Henry himself was a good deal of a prig) I might have written Dutch for the rest of my life, and then I should have stayed in Holland and a fat chance I should have had to survive when the Nazis came. I thought of the last list of their victims which the *Knickerbocker News* had brought me the day before, and in which as usual I had found the names of several sons of old friends, for the swine were now exterminating the younger generation. I cursed them under my breath.

Willem looked up. "Anything bothering you, Father?" he asked.

"No, I was just thinking of my sister's elder son and was wondering whether she was still alive. Of course, I told you that my last surviving uncle died too a few months ago and . . ."

"Father," said my son, who sometimes reverses the roles and assumes the parental position, "we simply can't let you go on

---

* Grace Castagnetta, the pianist, and HvL's collaborator in several words-and-music books.

like this. It will kill you, and we want to keep you for just as long as we can. You are a funny fellow, but a pretty good one, as they come, even as a father, and we want to keep you. . . ."

"Thank you, Son, but these things happen. They are all gone now. My old sister was the last one, and I can only hope that she is out of her misery. These things are harder to take than I thought."

"Yes, and what can you do about them?"

"Not a damn thing!"

"Then write it out of your system. You are much more fortunate than the rest of us."

"What do you mean?"

"You can write it out of your system. And when you get tired of writing, you can draw it out of your system, and, if nobody is listening, you can fiddle it away."

"I know, but hell and damnation, what shall I write next? I am going crazy. I can't make up my mind. I have so many ideas that are good. I just can't decide, and another month of this sort of thing and I shall take to drink or to reading Proust, or I shall write a life of Walt Whitman with a dedication to the spirit of democracy."

"No, Father, please! Not that! No, not that!"

"Well, then, how shall I save myself?"

"By using this little story of your Franciscan friend as a general introduction for your autobiography, for the sort of autobiography at which you hinted in the introduction to the part I have read, a book containing all the ideas and things the boys in camp want to know about. Use that brainful of history of yours to help these poor kids out and make the world a little less strange and terrible than it is. You should know them as I have come to know them now, after living with them for a year and a half. They are completely lost, and you sit like some old, fat Montaigne (though I will say that you seem to have lost a lot of weight and you look much the better for it—

keep it up) and you could help them no end and you won't. You've got scruples about writing about yourself. Forget about them. If you hate so much telling about yourself, keep all that part down as much as you can, but use the rest as so many pegs and hang your ideas on them like the clothes in your closet. Start out with this little prologue in heaven and tell these poor kids the truth, for everybody seems to be lying to them. Why, you ought to see the stuff. . . ."

But he never got further than that, for at that moment something happened. It was not quite a revelation. It was not serious enough for that. But like a bolt out of the blue (I think that is the expression) an idea came to me, so startling and so simple and so absolutely and completely what I wanted that it made me jump out of my chair as if I had been stung by that wasp which for the last three days had been buzzing around in my room.

"Good Lord!" Willem shouted. "What has happened now? What have I done?"

"Only this, my beloved son. You have given me the answer to all those things that were driving me crazy."

"How?"

"I don't know. By something you said, I suppose, but I've got it! I've got it! I've got it!"

"Got what?"

"That damn book! The book I should write next. I even have the title, and what a title! A honey! Even Max * won't be able to find a better one, though of course he will try. What a fool I was never to have thought of it before, and now out of the mouths of babes and . . ."

"Never mind. I know the rest, and please remember I'm an officer now and a gentleman by act of Congress, too. But what is the title?"

---

* M. Lincoln Schuster, of the firm of Simon and Schuster.—Ed.

"*Report to Saint Peter.*"

"What do you mean?"

"Everything I had been looking for. Someday I shall have to go and interview Saint Peter about the possibilities of having just such a little garden as that of Saint Francis. Some friendly place full of flowers and birds where I can entertain my friends. I shall have to fill out all kinds of documents, for with all those New Deal boys there . . ."

"Forget about them," Willem interrupted. "New Deal boys don't go to heaven. God doesn't like them. They're always bothering him with their pamphlets about how he should really run the world and they're trying to organize the angels and make them ask for time and a half when they have to entertain visiting Baptists."

"Son, please don't be ribald about the only occasion your father has had serious business with heaven."

"Okay. But tell me the rest."

"I will. In this book, I shall write just as the name implies. I shall write it as if it were the report I meant to take with me when I have to go and see Saint Peter and when, instead of filling out all those endless blanks he will hand me, I shall just say, 'With your permission, Your Reverence or Your Excellency (or whatever you are supposed to say), here is everything you could ever possibly want to know about me. Every idea I have ever had. Everything I have ever thought upon pretty damn near (pardon me) every subject. It is like the essays of that Monsieur de Montaigne of whom you must have heard, for most likely he is right in there on the other side of the gate. He told the world that no matter what it might say about his stuff, it would have to confess that he had written in complete good faith. I have tried very hard to do the same, Your Honor, so if you will kindly have a look at it, you won't have to waste time on all these formulas and blanks (I never know what to do with them anyhow), and then, if you will let me come back in a couple of days and will kindly let me have your answer, it will make everything much simpler for you and do away with all the red tape.' "

"A charming idea," my son agreed, "but what will you do with yourself all that time? Saint Peter is a pretty old gentleman by now, and he may not read so fast as you do, or he may mislay the book and forget about it and you may have to wait the better half of eternity."

"That is very simple. I shall go to that little garden of the good Francis. He will hardly order me out. He had much too good a time when he visited us in Veere, and I shall be very quiet and ask for nothing."

"And what will you do all that time to keep yourself amused?"

"I shall sit and think back to all the good things I had in life —to all the people I loved—to that marvelous adventure which was life."

"And you will wait for me?"

"Of course I will. But please do me one favor. Come as late as you can."

"I will, and now I must go and pack. I have got to be back in camp before eleven tonight."

And while my son was putting his things together, I took a clean sheet of the old and trusted yellow paper and on it I printed in clear, bold letters

REPORT TO SAINT PETER

and then I started on the rest—all of which you will find in the remaining pages of this book.

CHAPTER I

The Circumstances Under Which I Made My Appearance on This Earth

February 9, 1943

I was born on the fourteenth of January of the year 1882. I do not know whether or not Venus was in the ascendant on that fateful night, nor have I the vaguest notion in what part of the heavens Capricorn and Ursa Major were disporting themselves with Ishtar. I realize the great role astrology has played in history from the days of the original cave man to those of his descendant, Adolf Hitler. I have carefully studied and tried to make sense of the horoscopes which Johannes Kepler drew up for the Duke of Wallenstein and for the Emperor Matthias. But I feel about astrology the way I do about palmistry, numerology, bibliomancy, sciomancy, haruspicy, myomancy, orniscopy, geomancy, gastromancy, stichomancy, dactyliomancy, capnomancy, and progressive education.

I don't want to say that there is nothing to them. A great many people brighter than I have found solace and comfort in studying the flights of birds, the lines in their hands, the behavior of mice, the way the smoke would rise from the chimney, or the way a cock would pick up grains. But I have listened to their learned arguments in the same spirit of doubt as descends upon me like a fog the moment some ardent disciple of Nostradamus tries to convince me that this French physician was something more than a clever charlatan and that his prophecies about the Emperor Napoleon and the disastrous tidal wave of Lisbon were something more than the usual abracadabra of the necromancer's trade of the early half of the sixteenth century.

Some fifteen years ago, when the Period of the Great Nonsense was making the whole world rich and when the speculators, for lack of better information, were asking the stars to tell them whether U.S. Steel would go up twenty points the next day, or fall thirty, and when a mysterious person by the name of Evangeline Adams was the confidante of our Great Men of Business, one of the sisters of the great Brotherhood of Star-Gazers prevailed upon me to find out something definite about the exact hour at which I had made my appearance on this planet.

I duly wrote to one of my aunts who had been present at this occasion, and she informed me that it was shortly after three o'clock of the night of January 14, in the year of grace 1882, and that the doctor, after a long struggle with this most obstinate newcomer, said, "Well, he seems all safe and sound, but God save me from another night like this, for the brat must weigh at least nine pounds."

That happened, of course, in the old days when respectable housewives still bore their children in the seclusion of their own homes, and, as no hospital scales were ready at hand, my weight was merely guessed at by the midwife (for midwives still assisted physicians and often knew much more than the regular leech). But the subsequent development of this sprawling infant into a creature well over six feet two and weighing (in spite of all sorts of dietetic experiments) approximately 285 pounds makes me shiver whenever I think of what my poor mother must have suffered before at last, after hours of suffering, she was told that it was a boy and that he looked like his father.

This has always struck me as a most unfair arrangement.

For I loved my mother but never had any sincere affection for my father. The reason for this dislike will become abundantly clear to the reader long before he has reached the middle of this volume. He will then understand why I never liked my face. For, from a very early age, I tried to separate myself completely from my paternal parent, but, try as I might, I could never get rid of the imprint he had left upon my eyes and nose and the shape of my mouth. This, incidentally, will explain why I have but small love for mirrors and photographs. Both tell me something of which I want to be reminded as little as possible. And this aversion has gone so far that when occasionally a sincere lover of one of my books asks me for a photograph, I will send him a picture, not of my face but of my hands, for those hands are the hands of my mother.

That, I think, is about all there is to report about the fourteenth of January of the year 1882. The house in which I was born no longer exists. It disappeared during that bombing of Rotterdam by means of which the Nazis intended "to teach a lesson to the rest of the world." The stones have since been carted away to reconstruct parts of Cologne and Hamburg after the RAF got through with them. The street has been incorporated into a new city plan which no longer follows the pattern of the ancient and honorable town of Rotterdam.

The archives of my native town too went up in smoke when the Nazis indulged in their first great manifestation of mass sadism (there have been dozens of others since then, and worse), and so there is nothing left to bear witness to the fact that I actually exist except for myself and a copy of the *Nieuwe Rotterdamsche Courant* for Sunday, the fifteenth of January of the same year. This document, for some mysterious reason, found its way into a tin box in which, some thirty years ago, I deposited some of my mother's letters and other documents of a personal nature and which came back to the light of day when (in anticipation of another war) I evacuated all my books and belongings from a storehouse in Middelburg and had them sent out to Old Greenwich.

The leading story of this four-page sheet is devoted to "a new sensational process in London," where it seems that a certain George Henry Lamson, being in urgent need of money, poisoned his brother-in-law, Percy Malcolm John, who was worth $15,000 and who was known to have arranged that, in the case of his death, one half of this sum would go to his sister, the loving wife of aforementioned George Henry Lamson. Quinine mixed with aconite did the trick. It would not have worked in normal cases, but poor Percy Malcolm John, having always been an invalid, easily succumbed to the action which the aconite exercised upon his weak heart and lungs and soon fell into a coma. But not before someone who helped carry him to his bed (he was complaining of a severe stomach-ache) heard him whisper, "It's that damn brother-in-law of mine, and this time he's got me."

Unfortunately, there the report about the "latest sensational process in London" ended, and, not having access to any of the London papers of the subsequent week, I don't know what happened to the "damn brother-in-law." But the English correspondent of the *Rotterdamsche Courant* did not doubt for a moment that English justice would promptly be meted out to this cunning criminal and that before the passage of another fortnight he would have been hanged by the neck.

The rest of the paper was devoted to such news as was supposed to interest those good citizens of Rotterdam who were sufficiently faithful in their observance of the Calvinist Sabbath not to waste their time reading "wicked worldly literature." There was a lengthy report from the commander of the Polar expedition ship, the *Willem Barendse,* about his fourth visit to the waters around Jan Mayen Island, recently come to a most successful conclusion. Then there was a report about "Child Delinquency" in which terrible predictions were made

about what would happen unless something was done to put
an end to these "scandalous outbreaks against order and discipline." An unfortunate private in The Hague, P.J.T., aged
twenty years, who claimed that his duties as a true Christian
made it impossible for him to wear the King's uniform and
train to become the murderer of his fellow men, was condemned to three months' detention and to six months of
service in a special battalion of hard military labor. One happy
citizen was allowed to accept the insignia of an *officier de
l'Académie Française* accorded him by His Excellency the
French Minister of Public Education. The Scheveningen fishermen had gone on strike, and a gentleman in Amsterdam had
received a letter in which an anonymous correspondent had
threatened that he would burn down his house unless he at
once received fifty guilders. Through the diligent researches
of the ever-watchful Amsterdam police, the culprit had soon
been detected and had proved to be a former colonial soldier
and a cousin by marriage of the recipient of the threatening
letter.

Then there were a great many ships which had either arrived or departed. A steam dredge had safely arrived at the
island of Curaçao to widen the harbor of Willemstad. The
demand for coffee was "calm"; that for tea, a little better.
Petroleum, the day before, had been quoted on the New York
Exchange at 67⁄8c. and in Philadelphia at 67⁄8c., but there
would not be any hope for an improvement in the present
unsatisfactory prices until the speculators once more saw a
chance to make a decent profit.

According to a Reuter telegram from Paris, Léon Gambetta
had delivered a speech in the Chamber of Deputies about a
planned revision of the French Constitution. Vienna's Reuter
man told how Turkey was trying to gain the support of Germany and Austria in the current Egyptian and African ques-

tion and of a lively exchange of views among the chancelleries of Rome, Vienna, Berlin, and Constantinople.

In distant Palermo a limited company had been formed for the purpose of building a railroad to the top of Mount Etna, and an irate citizen wrote a letter to the editor of the paper about the necessity of maintaining the equivalent of a five-cent fare for even the outlying districts of the city. The German opera was giving a performance of *The Huguenots,* and the Royal French Opera from The Hague was giving *Lucia di Lammermoor.* Dr. Maurice Son, D.D.S. (according to the new law), offered his services daily from nine in the morning until eight at night, and his colleague, Dr. Beich, also offered to pull and fill, but he apparently did not keep such hideously long hours as his rival and contented himself with saying that he was in his office "every day." Other medical items of interest were provided by an advertisement of a series of popular works on "The ordinary household cold and its care," by Dr. Niemeyer, who was also responsible for a translation from the German of an opus entitled, *The Child: Hints and Suggestions for Mothers.* A husband and wife, both of them speaking foreign languages, hoped to see themselves placed as steward and stewardess on a steamer "plying the domestic harbors." A master pastrycook was looking for a second assistant, Roman Catholic and unmarried, and a public benefactor in Amsterdam (Damrak 26) offered tickets in a lottery, in which one could not possibly lose and which guaranteed the happy participants 400,000 francs each month.

An angel, carrying an enormous bottle, drew attention to "Tooth Angel"—the remedy that would immediately make even the worst of toothaches disappear, and elegant Ladies' Felt Slippers were offered at only a guilder twenty-five, while "cloth-bottom shoes according to the latest style" went for only five guilders fifty. An elaborate advertisement for music boxes, written in German, was made doubly interesting by having half of its contents printed upside down, and a new bank had been founded and was looking for an additional half-million guilders. The Singer Manufacturing Company of New York offered its latest machines for only one guilder a week, or eighteen guilders straight if one preferred to pay cash. Someone was in the market for an iron factory chimney. A Mr. J. A. Weinbeck, specialist in feasts, offered to enrich any party with his delightful bits of verse and his irresistible jokes and surprises. A dozen maritime enterprises, duly giving the names of the captains of their vessels, announced the forthcoming sailings of, among others, the *Hallanshire* (400 tons), the *Demetrius* (380 tons), and the *Condor* and the *City of Rotterdam* (both of 700 tons) to Semarang, Surabaya, Glasgow, and Christiania (ice permitting), and somewhere at the bottom of page two there appeared a two-line item informing a world already so full of a number of things that Mrs. E. J. van Loon-Hanken had given birth to a son.

Some twenty years ago, when I was in one of my philosophical moods (those moods which make the family say, "We wish Pa would snap out of it and be funny again!"), I got fascinated by the problem of the effect of environment upon personality and diligently searched Dr. Ploetz's well-known epitome of history to see whether I could perhaps discover an event (any event at all) that had taken place at the very moment I had seen the light of the moon (for the meteorological news service of the newssheet stated definitely that it had been a fine moonlit night on the fourteenth of January). But the year 1882, I found, was one of the most prosaic periods of which record has been preserved for mankind's benefit. A short while later, while rather aimlessly perusing a life of Richard Wagner, I came upon the information that Wagner had finished his drama *Parsifal* a few hours before I had been born. I failed, however, to see any connection between these two events. God knows I have been a good deal of a fool, but hardly a pure fool, and the Grail to the quest of which I have devoted my life is very different from the crater from which the Lord was supposed to have drunk His wine during the last evening He spent with His disciples.

Of Rotterdam, the Town in Which I Was Born

THE NAZIS have made things easy for posterity. The people of Rotterdam were never given to any exuberant love of the arts. They have systematically neglected the few literary men born in their city. Erasmus, of course, had his statue (the Germans let it melt down during the great conflagration they started by their bombardment), but that bronze effigy was more the result of outside pressure than of local enthusiasm. Since to most people outside of the Netherlands Rotterdam was chiefly known as the birthplace of the most learned man of his day and age, it would never have done if distinguished foreigners on a pilgrimage to this holy site had had to be sent away without a single postal card of their beloved Desiderius. As for the other literary statue erected to a native son, it stood (and for all I know, may still stand) in the park and bore the name of Hendrik Tollens (1780-1856). No use looking him up in your encyclopedia, for he is not there. He was an amiable old gentleman who combined the business of being a grain merchant with that of writing reams of highly patriotic literature. One of his poems was somehow elevated to the rank of the national anthem. It is a pretty sad piece of doggerel, but you know how those things are. Francis Scott Key, by any other standard than that of the emotions, was not exactly a Shakespeare either, yet he lives, and even his fellow Baltimoreans have finally accepted him as one of their own. And so Hendrik

Chapter II

Tollens had his statue, carved out of marble by local subscription. But whether the burghers of my native town contributed because Tollens, although "in grain," had always met all his commitments on the dot or whether they felt a sincere love for him

Whose veins are filled with pure Dutch blood
Untouched by foreign strain,

that I could not tell. Maybe it was a little of both.

There were a few rather good tombs in the Big Church, but those had been erected over the last resting places of half a dozen seventeenth-century admirals who had contributed to Holland's commercial prosperity of that age. They were the boys the Rotterdam people understood and appreciated.

But when it came to artists, fellows with long hair and velvet coats and a constitutional indifference towards the paying of bills—that was something else again. And therefore I doubt whether my native town would ever have felt compelled to place a memorial tablet on the façade of the house in which, on that very dark night of January fourteenth, 1882, I saw the light of day. However, as I said a moment ago, Herr Hitler has saved them from any such obligation, for that house, together with practically the whole of the old town, was completely destroyed when the Luftwaffe, hours after the surrender of the city, swooped down upon the helpless populace, shot and burned some ten thousand men, women, and children to death, and left the town a shambles.

Thus, all that remains of the house of my birth is a hole in the ground. It is a vast network of cellars, which undoubtedly have been so filled with debris that they have lost all their old charm and curiosity as the remnants of the medieval cloister which was the first edifice to be erected in that part of the marshes on the right bank of the river Rotte, which subsequently gave its name to the settlement built along its shores.

Report to Saint Peter

These cellars are among my earliest recollections. I knew that they existed ever since the day (I must have been about four years old) when I wandered out of the kitchen and lost myself in the darkest darkness I had ever perceived. I set up such a howl of fright that I was soon rescued, but the cook improved the occasion by telling me all about the extent of these terrible subterranean caverns which, according to her account, covered so vast an amount of territory that several bad little boys, who had dared to visit them without their parents' permission, had never again been found until years afterwards, when their skeletons, gnawed white by the rats, had again been brought to the surface of the earth. Years afterwards I discovered that this story had been considerably exaggerated. The yawning space underneath our house was indeed of somewhat unusual dimensions, but I never found out who had been originally responsible for these excavations. It pleases my historical sense (and I was born with a terrific love for the glamour of the past) to imagine that these cellars had been constructed for the benefit of the Dominicans, who undoubtedly had had a cloister of their order on or near the spot where I was born. But many years later, when I came to know something about the earliest history of Rotterdam, I learned that the problem was a little more complicated than I had expected.

There are no early maps of what today is the second biggest city of the Kingdom of the Netherlands, but for that matter there are very few early representations of any of the big Dutch towns. The reason is a very simple one. Those cities themselves were of comparatively recent origin and did not come into their own until after the Dutch had thrown off the Spanish yoke and had invested in the Indian trade the money they had made in the herring business. Then at last they had been able to afford printing presses and engraving establishments of their own; but during the sixteenth century they were still overgrown villages, situated in some convenient spot where they

could also act as market places for the more immediate hinterland. And most of the early plans of these cities were therefore made in Nuremberg or were the work of some enterpris-
ing Italian publisher. For in the early half of the sixteenth
century the world was as much interested in geography as it is
today in radio and flying.

Those who were obliged to remain at home wanted to know
all about the rest of the planet, and there were fortunes to be
made in books about travel and about foreign lands. In due
course of time, the Low Countries got their share, and their
cities were duly described and, if of any importance at all, were
honored with a double-page picture. These pictures, however,
were never done on the spot. We now know how those early
Italian and South German publishers worked. They employed
two kinds of artists—a few first-rate craftsmen stayed at home
and did the actual engraving, while others of a slightly inferior
caliber were sent abroad to provide the office with the rough
sketches their more efficient brethren needed for the finished
product.

By and large, these scouts were pretty close observers, but in
many instances they seem to have done what the traveling boys
of our Currier and Ives did. When it came to certain details of
the town they were depicting, it seems that they merely indicated with a few scrawls or a penciled note what they meant to
convey to the man at home: "here a castle" or "harbor full of
boats" or "cowsheds and vegetable gardens" or "put in a few
trees." Today we have to reconstruct our ancient cities from
these charming-looking but not exactly scientific plans, and
this leads to all sorts of difficulties.

I have most carefully compared all the earliest maps of
Rotterdam and now think that I have a fairly clear idea of what
the spot where I was born must have looked like when my great-
great-great-grandfather exchanged a somewhat embarrassed
"Good morning to you" with the cleric who was supposed to

be the father of that little Gerrit Gerritszoon boy whose mother was in domestic service and therefore should have been a little more careful than she was. Just one little boy born outside of wedlock might have been overlooked, but two of them in rapid succession was a little too much, and it was just as well for the community at large that these little bastards had now been sent to their mother's relatives in near-by Gouda, and to hope to God they never came back!

Well, then, it seems that the earliest part of Rotterdam had been built along the right bank of the river Rotte at the spot where that not very noble stream lost itself in the Maas. Why the river before Rotterdam was called the Maas, when it was really just as much part of the Rhine, is a puzzle I have never seen successfully solved, but it has been called the Maas since the beginning of time.

At one time, this was to prove a most inconvenient arrangement, which did immense damage to the whole of the Netherlands. In the year 1810 it gave Napoleon his chance to proclaim that since all this land was merely a vast accumulation of mud carried down by the Meuse (as the section of the Maas flowing through France is called), it therefore belonged to his empire. Whereupon he annexed it without any further ado as something that was his by natural right and plundered it so efficiently that it took the Dutch people almost a century to recover from the shock.

I shall have to return to this sad point, for that annexation also seems to have deprived my own family of the little glory it had, but I mention it here because otherwise the reader, who will continually hear me speak of the Maas, will say, "But on our map, it looks as if Rotterdam is situated on the Rhine and not on the Maas." And the reader is right except that in Rotterdam the Rhine has always been known as the Maas, and there's no use fighting the map.

Well, then, after the people of the fishing village on the

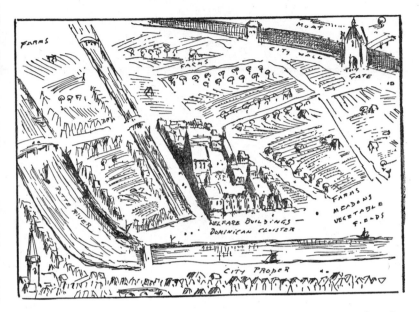

This is the sort of sketch from which the engraver in the publisher's office was supposed to do his work.

banks of the Rotte and the Maas had got permission from their overlords, the counts of Holland, to incorporate themselves as a "city" with regular civic rights, they must have built themselves a stone wall (that was the first thing people did in the Middle Ages after they had incorporated themselves as a town) and, because they expected a speedy growth of their newly founded establishment, they included a great deal of unimproved real estate along the left bank of the Rotte so that they would have space in which to grow as more and more natives of the surrounding countryside hastened to this safe enclosure, where they might enjoy the benefits of living under the protection of a prosperous new center of business and enterprise.

Then as now, the magistrates who were in charge of the public's welfare liked to keep the establishments connected with the highly necessary but rather unpleasant aspects of their civic life out of sight and at a safe distance from the center of the town. And, since the city seemed to be moving southward and westward in the general direction of the water front, such establishments as the hospitals, the home for the lepers, the dungeons for the more dangerous lunatics, the reform schools for juvenile and female delinquents, the morgue, and the orphan asylum were removed to the left bank of the Rotte and formed a complex which more or less maintained its character for several hundred years.

The original town hall, erected in the same neighborhood, still fulfilled its ancient function when I was born, and I spent the first seven years of my life right opposite what was supposed to be its façade. It was then a rather prosaic building, having been completely overhauled in the 1830's and, according to the taste of the time, given the aspect of a Greek temple. I never saw anything of all those ancient houses which for so many years must have harbored the sick and the deformed and the lepers and the lunatics and all the other flotsam and jetsam of a medieval community which lived in a swamp, was subject to all kinds of scourges and epidemics, and could pride itself upon a death rate which put the average life expectancy at thirty years, so that one had to be in a mighty hurry to accomplish anything at all. At the same time, however, the existence of this "welfare city" for the benefit of those who were unable to look after themselves showed that the townspeople were very deeply conscious of their duties towards the less fortunate members of the community.

The Reformation did away with the old belief in the efficacy of good works. Dr. John Calvin's hideous doctrine of predestination—the belief that God, from the very beginning of eternity, had preordained all men to either everlasting happiness or misery in the hereafter—gave man no chance to try and make up for his past deficiencies by exerting himself in the right direction and by squaring accounts with the Lord.

Old John Calvin (who was to become one of my pet abominations) would not stand for that sort of bribery of the Almighty. You were either foreordained to salvation or you went to hell, and all you could do was to hope for the best. I lived the greater part of my life underneath the shadow of this damnable doctrine, but I am glad to say that a great many of my neighbors, even if they proclaimed themselves devout followers of the sour-visaged French reformer from Geneva, never allowed practice to interfere too seriously with theory. The medieval belief in good works as a way of gaining grace had been too strongly ingrained into their very being to be driven out completely. Although they might spend all their days worrying quietly about the fate that awaited them, they still felt that they were not only their brothers' keepers but that they also owed a duty towards those who, by the misfortunes that haunted them at every step, proved in unmistakable fashion that they were not among the "elect." And although the cities and villages of the old Dutch Republic were ruled without a vestige of democracy, the rich merchants who thought that

God had called upon them to be the undisputed masters of their bailiwicks never ceased to have an appropriate feeling of responsibility.

The lame, the halt, and the blind, the sick of body and mind, and those too old or too young to take care of themselves were, if not bountifully, at least decently taken care of. And for those self-respecting poor who would have died rather than accept charity, there were the so-called *béguinages* (*Begijnerhof* in Dutch) where every respectable old lady could have her own little home and where she could meet death surrounded by her own furniture, her own mementos of a happier day, and her own cat.

As all these unfortunate people needed a certain amount of care and as the social service of the Middle Ages was a monopoly of the Church, it was quite natural that the *béguinage* should have been built around a monastery. In our case—in my native city—it had been a Dominican monastery. This had been re-built and enlarged in the year 1444 but had been destroyed by the big fire of 1563, which ruined the greater part of Rotterdam and gave rise to the ordinance requiring that henceforth houses should be (if possible) of brick rather than wood and positively forbidding the use of thatched roofs for the houses that stood inside the city walls.

After that period (the end of the sixteenth century) thatched roofs disappeared from practically all Dutch villages and towns and were replaced by the red and blue tiles which added such pleasantly picturesque detail to the Dutch landscape.

After Rotterdam went over to the side of the Reformation, this Dominican cloister disappeared. The "preacher men"—as the monks were generally known among the populace (for the "dogs of the Lord" specialized in evangelistic labors and were among the best speakers of the Middle Ages)—deprived of their old home and a chance of keeping alive by their labors, fled to God knows where or made their peace with the new dispensation and became small artisans. And their former premises were converted into a brewery and afterwards into a gin factory.

As for the different charitable institutions that had been entrusted to their care, these too, one after the other, disappeared. The plaguehouse became a superfluous luxury, for, with the general improvement in hygiene, the disease became more and more rare and finally disappeared altogether. Leprosy too became so scarce that it was no longer necessary to keep a special hospital in which the patients could be segregated. A more humane conception of lunacy frowned upon the old method of locking poor demented creatures up in ill-ventilated cellars. Unless they were actually a menace to themselves and their neighbors, they were allowed to live with their relatives or were boarded out by the municipality among the poorer families, who in this way made a few extra pennies. The orphans, as prospective communicants of the Church, became an object of special care to the new clergy and were located in more appropriate quarters, though it is curious to note how little sense of hygiene the good people of the sixteenth century had. For a while, these children were made to live in the old plague hospital and afterwards in a discarded church. And so gradually, one after another of these old eleemosynary establishments was either pulled down or converted into storehouses or factories.

By the time I was born, these buildings had been so often changed and overhauled that no one of them bore any resemblance to what they had been three centuries before. But no matter how often it had been repaired and reconstructed, the part of the city in which they were located still retained a great deal of the rabbit-warren aspect it must have had in the beginning.

That, of course, is no particularly brilliant observation. Unless a town is completely destroyed, as Rotterdam has since then been destroyed by the Nazis, it will always bear the imprint of its original settlement. In Paris, if you are fortunate enough to have an acquaintance who knows the history of the old Lutetia Parisiorum, you can easily reconstruct the provincial capital that Julian the Apostate called his "dear Lutetia" and where Saint Denis first preached Christianity to the long-haired citizens. Ever since I wrote my life of old Piet Stuyvesant I have been able to follow the original map of Nieuw Amsterdam as easily as that of our beloved Veere, where the number of inhabitants had shrunk from seven thousand in the late Middle Ages to a mere eight hundred and something, and where less than one twentieth of the former houses remain erect.

I don't know what Stalin has done to Moscow, but the great fire of the Napoleonic invasion in 1812, although it destroyed the greater part of the old city, did not change it very noticeably from what it was like when Ivan III (the contemporary of Columbus) sent for a group of Italian architects to turn his capital into a "modern city."

But the most curious experience along this line I ever had was in Les Baux, in southern France. I don't know how many of my readers have ever visited this curious rocky city, the lords of which were once rulers of Constantinople and which for several hundred years was the center of the brilliant life of Provence. Nothing much remains of all this ancient glory, but I knew a British sculptor who had lived there for years and who knew every scrap of that small plateau which dominated all the surrounding landscape. He once took me to a field and asked me whether I saw anything unusual. I said no, just a bit of neglected meadow. Then he pointed to a row of low tree stumps, which still showed signs of life. Les Baux, as far as he had been able to make out, had been a spot of prehistoric worship long before the coming of the Romans. Those stumps were the descendants in the nth degree of the trees which had lined the road that led up to the prehistoric place of worship on the edge of the rock. Once one was able to see them as such, the entire plan of this prehistoric establishment became clear.

Afterwards the Greeks came, and then the Romans and the different tribes that overran Provence, which, as the direct heir to the culture of the Greeks, had for centuries been the center of European civilization. Each succeeding group of invaders pulled down what the others had erected before them, and finally the artillery of Richelieu reduced the whole town to a mass of ruins. Just the same, it had started as a prehistoric settlement and it still showed unmistakable signs of its origin. And in the same way, the neighborhood in which I was born, though everything had been rebuilt a number of times during the last three hundred years, still retained the aspects of what it had been in the beginning—a cloister surrounded by all kinds of buildings devoted to charitable purposes, and not constructed according to a preconceived plan but added to from time to time as certain needs made themselves felt.

And this original character clung to the entire neighborhood. Our house too was a crazy quilt of rooms and staircases. No two rooms were on the same floor. Short and long staircases ran every which way. My own little room (as soon as I was allowed to enjoy such a luxury) seemed to hang suspended in mid-air, for the space below it belonged to another house. The kitchen was two staircases below the living room, which also (as was customary in those days) was used as a dining room. The back windows of that dining room looked out upon a courtyard which was not our own but which must have been part of the old cloister garden. The enormous attic was a double-decker, which showed that once upon a time (when merchants still lived over their own stores) it must have been used as storage space for linen or cheese or God knows what. And as for the forest of chimneys which stuck out high over the roofs,

I never found out which ones were ours and which belonged to our neighbors.

It was therefore a place which could not fail to frighten a small child, and, as I have always been of a timorous character, I suffered a great many agonies when in the evening, my candle in hand, I was told to be a brave boy and go up to my room alone.

There was one spot I feared most of all. That was where the steps to my own cubbyhole led off from the main staircase. The wall opposite this junction was covered with a large mirror. Now somebody for my Sint Niklaas had given me a picture book with a terrible-looking goblin in it. And a maid, instructed to see me off to bed, had told me that if the clock should strike just at the moment I passed that mirror, that particular goblin would jump out of it and bite me. Of course, servants and nurses who do that sort of thing should be shot, but how were my parents to know? Surely I would never tell them, realizing that I should be laughed at for my troubles and should be called a coward and a scary little infant. And so, night after night, my heart beating violently with fear, I would creep past that mirror, hoping that perchance the clock would not strike at that precise moment and let the goblin get me.

And then there were nights when there was a fire. Unbelievable as it may sound, even during the eighties of the last century the second biggest city of the Netherlands did not have a professional fire department. The business of fighting an almost weekly conflagration (and the town with all its storehouses was highly inflammable) was left to an amateur corps of fire fighters. Many attempts had been made to change this deplorable state of affairs, but to no avail. There was a considerable premium for the fire engine which was able to "give water" first of all at the scene of disaster. The competition for this sum of money was so great that, in the run to the danger spot, it was quite common for these small man-hauled fire engines to be upset, in which case the others raced merrily across the prostrate bodies of their less fortunate rivals that they might claim the right of having been the first to "give water."

In order to give this absurd arrangement some kind of standing, it was presented as a manifestation of the "good old civic spirit." Every citizen was supposed to do his share, but of course, in a class-ridden country like my native land, the thing had to be done in such a way that the gentry and the common people did not interfere too much with each other. Every engine had its own firemaster, recruited from the gentlemen living in that particular neighborhood, while those who pulled the contraption and did the pumping were of a somewhat lower social standing.

The difference between the two was definitely established by the fact that the firemaster wore a sash of the colors of Rotterdam's coat of arms, the green and white which you still see around the smokestacks of the vessels of the Holland-America Line. He also sported a long stick adorned with the same colors. With this stick he was supposed to smash the windowpanes of the houses into which the intrepid fire fighters were to break before they could tackle their intermural job.

As the great majority of the conflagrations then as now were fairly innocent affairs—a careless smoker and a mattress, or a dirty chimney—I don't know exactly how much use they could ever make of their staff of office. But every family was proud of having a few such historical relics among its ancestral heirlooms, and I am sorry I did not save the one that had belonged to my father, for it would have reminded me of one of the few qualities in my father's make-up for which I admired him. His fire company did have his interest, and no matter what the time of day or night, whether it was raining, snowing, or sleeting, the moment there was a fire alarm he was out in the street to unlock the near-by firehouse (a modest stone edifice holding two of the breed) and would last be seen galloping proudly away at the head of his men.

If I am not mistaken, when I grew a little older there were also a few engines, operated by means of steam and pulled by horses, but those made their appearance only on formal occasions, when the hand-driven pumps proved to be inadequate. Most of the citizens held them a little *infra dig.*—an innovation possibly efficient but not quite fair. In the same way the knights of the outgoing Middle Ages despised the use of gunpowder. It did the job all right, but gentlemen would not touch it, and, as a result, during the first fifty years after Berthold Schwartz's deplorable invention, anybody caught with a blunderbuss in his hands was invariably strung up from the nearest tree.

This was, of course, a perfectly normal reaction. Precisely the same thing happened twenty-five years ago, during World War I, when the Germans first used poison gas. Immediately a great many well-intentioned ladies and gentlemen wrote to the papers demanding that anybody using this "outrageous method of killing his enemies" be put up against a wall and shot. It was, of course, a hideous thing to be "gassed," and the victims suffered indescribable agonies. But the kind souls who were so thoroughly outraged by that particular kind of man's cruelty towards man can never have seen what shrapnel will sometimes do to a group of healthy youngsters caught in a hollow where the shrapnel reduces them to shreds.

The whole business of war is so foul that I am always a little surprised when people begin to differentiate between one method of tearing your opponent to pieces and another. They remind me of those rather naïve citizens who think of "nice diseases" and others that are not quite so nice and who treat the typhoid microbe with a certain degree of respect while they have only very harsh words to say about his colleagues who cause syphilis. That an illness is an illness, no matter in what guise it presents itself, is a fact they refuse to accept. Their curious religious tenets so profoundly affect their opinions that they are perfectly willing to co-operate in every method that will help stamp out horrible afflictions like leprosy or diphtheria but feel highly indignant if one approaches them on the subject of venereal diseases. These they wish to combat with moral precepts. Until microbes shall have become converted to Christianity, such efforts, I am afraid, will continue to be sad and disastrous failures. But this is a very old story, and I doubt whether anything much can be done about it until we shall have developed a new system of ethics not based upon the worship of a God of wrath and vengeance. At the moment of writing, it does not look as if this is likely to happen within the next couple of hundred years.

But I was talking about another though equally curious manifestation of that curious mental lethargy—that obstinate unwillingness to accept any kind of change which in the days of my youth continued to make the city of Rotterdam such a terrific fire hazard that it seems little short of a miracle that the city was not reduced to ashes at least half a dozen times during each of the six hundred years of its existence. Instead of copying the improvements in the fire-fighting methods of practically the whole civilized world, the citizens of Rotterdam stuck to the system that had come down to them from the Middle Ages. They had, of course, done away with the old bucket brigade which would have been no longer possible in a city where so many canals had been filled in to make room for the streets that could be used by horse-drawn traffic. They now used those fire engines which seem to have been a Dutch invention of the latter half of the seventeenth century, when the Dutch were the great pump experts of the world, being engaged in a gigantic effort to dry up in record time as many inland lakes as they could for the benefit of their rapidly increasing population. If the English had had those improved contraptions, the terrible London fire of 1666 might never have assumed the gigantic proportions it did. But, although everybody knew what those modern fire engines could do (they had been highly publicized in a series of magnificent etchings which Jan van der Heyden, a native of Gorinchem and therefore a fellow townsman of Pierre van Paassen, had made), they had at first been treated with as much suspicion as the automobile or the flying machine.

It so happened that during the seventeenth century the Dutch had been the most wide-awake of all nations, and fire engines as popularized by the excellent Jan van der Heyden had been introduced into every village and hamlet. But for as mysterious a reason as had made the Dutch the most progressive people of the seventeenth century, they had become the most hidebound nation of the next one. And I am sure that, when I was young, the fire engines used by the city of Rotterdam were either the original ones that had been bought two hundred years before or their first-generation descendants. They were rambling, rattling, clinking, crashing contrivances. They resembled miniature juggernauts, as we know them from the illustrations in our geography books. They had four small wheels, none of which showed the slightest desire to act in unison with any of the others. They were so low-slung that one expected them to be upset by the first unevenness in Rotterdam's abominably paved streets. Furthermore, they seemed to be as top-heavy as a houseboat and, as they were drawn by men and had no steering gear to keep them on an even keel, they wobbled all over the cobblestones and were always a grave menace to the little boys to whom a fire was the loveliest form of excitement of their rather boresome days.

Being a nicely brought-up little boy, I was never allowed to run after the fire engines, but on very rare occasions I would be fortunate enough to meet them just when they were coming

down one of the dikes, which, although they had been converted into streets, still stuck to their ancient character in being
much higher than the rest of the town. When the engines
rolled down these slight inclines, as many of the brave fire
fighters as could find room would hastily jump on board their
engine and coast down until they had once more reached the
level, when they were again obliged to get into harness, provided the ropes by means of which they pulled the monster had
not got themselves hopelessly tangled up in the wheels of the
engine, in which case five or ten minutes were lost unscram-
bling everything.

So far so good, and I loved all fires, as most small boys do.
But there was one thing connected with this form of civic
diversion which was the cause of some of the most unhappy
dreams of my childhood, and when one is very young, dreams
—especially nightmares—play a very important part in life.

During the Middle Ages, fires had been announced by the
ringing of one of the church bells. The ordinary bells for re-
minding the faithful that it was time for prayer or divine
service were never used for a fire warning. A special bell with a
very alarming, deep voice was set apart as a "fire bell," and it
was never rung unless the city was in a state of danger. But all
that had been changed during the period of the French administration, which had been oppressive but highly efficient.
There was to be no more bell ringing. The job of informing
the populace about the existence of a fire within their gates
was to be performed by the police. Every policeman was given
a little whistle. As soon as a fire had been discovered, he would
start tooting that damn thing, and the other policemen, hear-
ing him, would do likewise. Soon all the streets would be filled
by the dismal noise of something that resembled nothing quite
so much as very young and very sad calves bleating desperately
for their mothers.

I believe that those who have made a special study of the

very important subject of sleep inform us that we are very much mistaken when we claim that we had a dream that lasted for hours. Dreams, according to the professors, never last longer than a few seconds, if that long. They are probably right, but I remember distinctly that when those little tooters started to toot, I went through hours of agony before consciousness had again triumphed and I was allowed once more to return to that blessed state of nirvana which is one of God's greatest gifts to man. And during that period of misery, until I had at last returned to the realization that I was right there in my own little room with my pantaloons neatly folded over my shirt on the seat of my chair (as they should have been according to age-old custom) and with my father and mother asleep only a few steps away from my own door . . . during that eternity of despair I always had the same dream. The town of Rotterdam had been taken by the Spaniards, and I was listening to the shrieks of horror that accompanied the pillaging and murdering that were going on outside. Soon these horrors would reach our own premises, and then a heavy, iron-clad footstep on the stairs, a man with a long beak of a nose and black, piercing eyes, a dagger shining in the moonlight, a feeble shriek, and my small corpse would be thrown out of the window, to be loaded on a cart and dumped into the river.

How did I come by these hallucinations? How could I have helped not having them! Every day my mother took me for a walk. If the weather was bad, we stayed in the interior of the town, and I was sure (for it was only a step) to pass by the terrible House of a Thousand Fears. There was no doubt about its being that particular house, for a large picture in the front wall (done in colored tiles) explained everything that had happened there in full detail and in a most realistic fashion. This was the story.

When the Spaniards, infuriated at Rotterdam for having gone over to the cause of the rebellion, had submitted the city to one of those massacres with which Herr Hitler has once more made us so unhappily familiar, only the houses of the Catholics were spared. In order to set those apart from those inhabited by Protestants, a cross of blood was painted on the doors of those premises where the true faith was still being practiced. Now, one of the children of this particular domicile owned a little pet goat. His father had hastily slaughtered the poor creature and had used its blood to decorate the front door with the symbol of Holy Church. Then he and his family and friends had withdrawn into the cellar, where they had waited three whole days and nights until the fury of the Spanish hirelings had spent itself and they were once more able to return to the surface. In memory of these anxious hours, the place had become known as the House of a Thousand Fears, and it had been carefully preserved as an example of the brutality of bygone ages.

But in the year 1906, when I was in Russia for the Associated Press, I was to see similar crosses (only, in this instance they were Greek crosses and not Latin ones) on the doors of Polish huts in cities where the Czar's merry *soldatchiki* had broken the dullness of their life by arranging a couple of pogroms. In this case it was the Jews who were the victims and who had to kill their dogs and cats to provide themselves with the blood that was necessary to depict the cross of their enemies' Saviour.

I have it on unmistakable authority that this sort of sign painting has been revived during the present war at times when Adolf's supermen have gone on the warpath against the non-Aryan disturbers of the peace. All of which makes it difficult to be a historian and an optimist at one and the same time. But when I was six years old, such bestialities belonged so thoroughly to a past time which under no circumstances could ever come back that the horror they inspired was of a purely antiquarian nature. They made one feel very grateful for having been born in an era when such things were as much out of

The Pogrom

At night those stories of murder and bloodshed did not make a little boy of six sleep any the better.

the question as people being buried alive or burned at the stake for the sake of their religious convictions. To an imaginative child, however, they were a source of very unpleasant dreams, for they somehow associated themselves with the noise of the little horns blown by the police in case of a fire and thereupon created a perfect picture of invasion and massacre.

Another historical recollection that contributed to these nightmares was the poem (the first poem, I think, that I ever learned by heart) commemorating the mighty deeds of a local blacksmith who by his prodigious efforts had almost, but not quite, saved the town from being overrun by King Philip's famished and angry Swiss hirelings. For it would be unfair to put all the blame on the Spaniards. The generals and the higher officers of King Philip's army were Spaniards and Italians, but the rank and file were Swiss mercenaries, mountain boys who fought for pay and who did not care in what league they played so long as they could count on their monthly stipend and an occasional bonus in the form of a rich town offered to them for plunder.

It seems that when His Majesty's brave army, after a series of unexpected defeats, was forced to fall back upon Rotterdam or go without a roof over their heads or food in their bellies, this blacksmith, almost singlehandedly, had undertaken to hold the city gate against at least a thousand of the royal henchmen. According to contemporary reports, he had laid low at least fifty of these before he himself was overpowered and slain. The poem which stood engraved on a stone in the wall where the gate had been was of no great literary value, but it had a simple and easily remembered rhythm.

> *The mighty hammer of old Vulcan's child,*
> *To keep our city undefiled,*
> *Did mightily bash in the pates*
> *Of fifty of the tyrant's mates.*

I may not have got it exactly right and I can't look it up, as Herr Hitler is still on the premises, but I remember distinctly that it started out that way, and I was deeply impressed by that "mighty hammer of old Vulcan's child." I loved to watch the blacksmith just around the corner. In many respects, Rotterdam was still a good deal of a village, with horses being shod and the smith himself working where all could see and admire. To behold that bearded giant (a square beard was part of the regular getup of the members of that ancient and most honorable guild) twisting his red-hot iron into all sorts of forms and shapes, was the best entertainment the neighborhood had to offer. My interest in his activities may have been a direct reversion to the early Iron Age, when mankind, at last set free from its clumsy stone instruments, welcomed the introduction of iron weapons and tools with the eager satisfaction with which those of our own generation saw the coming of the age of electricity. Of course, at the age of six I did not yet bother myself with such thoughts. I loved to see this brawny fellow do his work because a serious illness at the age of four (some kind of typhoid fever) had left me a weak and puny child, and I compensated myself for my physical deficiencies by having an inordinate admiration for all those who could perform deeds of sinewy valor, whether it was twisting iron bars into hoops or carrying sacks of grain or lifting full-sized kegs of beer. Small wonder that the mightiest of them all, he who singlehandedly did "bash in the pates of fifty of the tyrant's mates," should have been one of my early heroes. But I paid the penalty for my too vivid imagination, for whenever the streets were filled with the moaning wails of those fire whistles, he too would come back to life and add to my agony by making me an eyewitness of those horrible crimes which once upon a time had been everyday incidents.

Those dreams no longer disturb me. I have seen worse since then—much worse and much less excusable. For I am writing this in August of the year 1943, and, while I am sitting at my desk, the radio is blaring forth the news about Germany's most recent outrage against the harmless and defeated Danes.

Must it always be that way? I think there is a solution, but that belongs in another chapter, still hundreds of pages removed from where we are now. And before I reach that final period of my life, a great many other things will have to happen, and one of those will deal with that most curious period when I began to pester my parents and my uncles (the uncles were much more sympathetic) about a question that bothered me at a very early age: what sort of people had we been before we became the kind of men and women we were then, with high hats and bustles, and going about our business as if the world had now achieved a state of perfection, the permanence of which nothing would henceforth disturb.

The Mummy in Its Case and the Stone Knives Which Had Been Dug Up Along the Seashore

SINCE THERE was nothing precocious about me, the reader will hardly expect that at the age of six or seven I should have indulged in Freudian pryings into sex and the origins of the human race. I was not submitted to any kind of sexual enlightenment until I was much older (twelve or thirteen) and then I got it in the usual nasty way, dubbed, however, the "nice way" by a generation which still believed that ignorance about these rather important matters was part of the blissful innocence of childhood. I accepted the existence of parents, uncles and aunts, grandpapas and grandmammas (I knew all of them well), and every other living being whom I met as something so normal that I never asked about the whence or how.

But there was the museum! Now Rotterdam, being essentially a commercial city, had neither much time nor much money to spare upon utterly useless pursuits, such as science, music, or the arts. Quite naturally, a Dutch town that had existed for more than five hundred years had accumulated a certain number of rather worth-while pictures. Rotterdam itself had not produced any of the great masters, but, as collecting paintings had been part of the more fashionable pattern of life, a sufficient number of citizens had acquired a sufficient number of landscapes and still lifes to warrant the existence of at least one small museum devoted to that particular form of art. It was located in an old building originally used as the administrative seat of one of the biggest of the near-by polders. (What those polders were I shall have to tell you later.) In the early forties of the last century, the polder needed larger quarters, and the old edifice was turned into a museum of art, or rather, it was continued as such, for the nucleus of a collection already existed. Needless to say, it had not been started by a native but by an import from the province of Limburg, a certain Mr. Boijmans, a lawyer by profession and a lover of art. In his honor, the name of the street on which his house was situated was changed from Meager Pig Market (there were two kinds of pig markets in all old Dutch cities—one for the fat pigs and one for the thin ones) to Boijmans Street, and as such it was known to all Rotterdam children. Not for its close association with the home of the Muses, but because, on the corner right opposite, was the kosher Jewish cakeshop, where they sold, for the sum of five cents, or one stiver, the largest and greasiest boluses to be had anywhere. The word *bolus* somehow fascinated me, for it was also used for something quite different (which all Dutch readers will understand). I shall not try to explain it to my American friends who went to Sunday school, were given pictures by Signor Sandro Botticelli at Christmas, and were told that while the Dutch school of the seventeenth century had undoubtedly produced some excellent craftsmen, the deplorable vulgarity of their subjects made them unfit for the purpose of ornamenting the walls of either the dining room or the parlor.

Afterwards, when I studied the tongue of Homer and Aeschylus, I learned that a *bolus* had meant a large clump of something or other. The honest Jewish baker (who unfortunately was always closed on Saturday, when we were free from school and had just received our weekly allowance of two stivers) gave value for our money, and blessed be his memory. I don't know what became of his popular establishment. Undoubtedly, a couple of Nazis first gorged themselves with all the sweet cakes they could eat (and according to reliable reports, they could eat incredible quantities) and then murdered the proprietor for the greater glory of Adolf Hitler and the Aryan race. Again I bless the baker's memory. He had the juiciest boluses I have ever encountered and thus deserved the gratitude of all little Rotterdam boys and girls of half a century ago.

I shall be much less enthusiastic about the collection of paintings that had found a home in the old residence of Mr. Frans Jacob Otto Boijmans. As I had started scribbling on every piece of paper that came near to my hand at a very early age (my sister, bless her heart! preserved a few specimens said to date from the third year of my life), I was supposed to have great promise as a painter: needless to say, as an "amateur painter," for the idea of having a painter in the family was about as popular as having a son who had gone in for business and who had achieved bankruptcy. In that case, however, the good people of Rotterdam would have understood how it had come about, for failure, in the legal sense of the word, with your belongings being sold in a tent in the street in front of your house, was a procedure with which they were only too familiar. But a lifetime spent in a garret in Paris was a prospect too horrible to contemplate. For decent families, of course, hid their artistic outcasts in the French capital, where people felt differently about such things and where an artist could subsist on a couple of guilders a week. When Papa or Grandpa died, the law insisted that these wayward children be present in person for the reading of the will. But such visits were cut as short as possible, for there always was a chance that in the meantime the crazy young man had got into a wild alliance with a grisette and might bring this creature along. Or even worse, he might actually have married her, in which case you had to treat her as a relative, and think of your poor mother being forced to welcome a daughter with a painted face and perhaps (most likely) a couple of children to call her *grand'-mère* instead of *oma*!

And so the idea of encouraging a youngster to emulate Rembrandt or Vermeer or that dreadful van Gogh boy (and his father a most respectable dominie) was definitely out, but a pleasant little gift for the pictorial arts was something else again. That could harm nobody, and it might bring about agreeable relationships with traveling English ladies and gentlemen (during the obligatory two-week trip to Germany or Switzerland in the summer), some of whom might prove to be profitable business acquaintances. I was therefore not only allowed to scribble to my heart's content, but also I was taken, at a very early age, to the temple of beauty that I might be inspired by the productions of our disreputable ancestors of the palette and brush.

Unfortunately, fifty years ago the art of cleaning pictures was still in its infancy, and, after two hundred years of neglect, peat fires, and candlelight, the masterpieces of the seventeenth century all looked as if they had been painted in chocolate. Those same pictures, which, when they had left the workshops of the masters, had been vibrant and clear, a joy to the eye for those who loved gaiety, were now a dull brown, and the layers upon layers of varnish with which the eighteenth and nineteenth centuries had covered them (to preserve them, as those fanatics of the varnish pot pretended to be doing, not knowing that in reality they were destroying them) had removed the last blotches of vermilion, blue, and white which had been the specialties of the contemporaries of Vermeer and Rembrandt. In consequence of which, the collection looked very much like the portraits of the defunct presidents and statesmen which grace the walls of the White House and give to that national shrine a dismal air that even the gilded piano of the East Room fails to dispel.

That piano, by the way, is just the sort of thing Mussolini would like, and if we don't shoot him after the war (and we probably won't, because he used to make the trains run on time) but send him to Madagascar or the Seychelles, we can let him have it for his parties, and his dear daughter Edda can play boogy-woogy for him whenever the spell comes upon him and he thinks he is back on the Piazza di Spagna with the people outside asking him for a speech.

Small wonder that a small boy was completely bored by this drab aggregation at the Boijmans Museum: ladies and gentlemen and dead fishes and rabbits, all of which reminded him of the faded carpet in his grandfather's bedroom. He vaguely understood that these pilgrimages to the museum of art had something to do with that worship of the ancestral glory which was part of his daily routine, but he fought those excursions by means of every form of sabotage known to a six-year-old until his parents decided that his love for drawing was not founded upon a serious basis but was of an amateurish nature, in which case it did not at all fit into the serious Dutch scheme of education. They thereupon discouraged his juvenile efforts with pen and pencil, for with his contempt for the "classics" he would never qualify for the examinations that would give him admission to the local drawing academy, and without a diploma from that institution one never could hope to become a "certified drawing teacher, holding both diplomas A and B and entitled to a government pension at the age of sixty."

So there was only one other solution: to set up as an independent artist—as an ordinary painter of pictures. And everybody knew what that led to—a garret, a dissolute life of sin, and a pauper's grave, after the best example of Rembrandt and his cronies.

My indifference, however, to portraits and still lifes of "pot

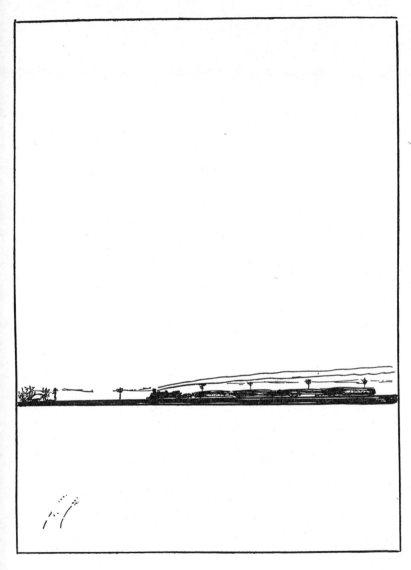

*At exactly three minutes of eleven that train would make
its appearance.*

and drapes" did not by any means indicate a total absence of curiosity about the world in which I lived. On the contrary. There was one museum in our town which had my most cordial approval and support. It bore the impressive title of Museum of the Knowledge of This Earth and Its People, Combined with Maritime Affairs. It had been a natural development in a city which ever since its beginning had been a center of world-wide trade. Sailors have always been collectors of exotic articles because circumstances have forced them into this queer practice. Suppose you returned from the Pacific and talked about a bird that was able to fold up its wings as if they had been parts of the blinds of a Dutch window. Your neighbors would have shrugged their shoulders and would have called you a liar until you returned with a nice stuffed albatross to show them that such a creature actually existed and that it did have a wingspread of more than sixteen feet. Or you returned from a Greenland whaling expedition full of stories about a people who were so densely covered up with furs that they looked as if they had no necks and carried their faces on their tummies. Nothing less than a full Eskimo suit of clothes would show the home folks that you had been telling the truth. A city like Rotterdam, therefore, was bound to become a veritable deposit of natural and ethnographic rarities.

Most of these souvenirs had been rubbish, for the average sailor of two or three centuries ago was not exactly a connoisseur, but here and there among these *objets de voyage* were treasures like those incomparable blankets of birds' feathers which the early whalers had brought back to New England and which there—of all things—had been used as sleigh blankets until rescued by people who recognized their beauty and value. Sometime during the middle of the last century a few discerning burghers of the good city of Rotterdam decided to save what could be salvaged from the local pawnshops and poorhouses and to exhibit those treasures, duly repaired and fumigated, for the benefit of those of their neighbors who still took an interest in such affairs. For, with the spread of enlightenment and the triumph of the steamship, the earth had lost a great deal of its former mystery and enchantment, and every little boy could now tell you, "The albatross, a bird belonging to the family of the Diomedea, is related to the petrel. *Diomedea exulans* of the Pacific is the best known of all the twenty species. It feeds upon fish and offal and, when gorged, may be unable to fly," and that, of course, knocked the bottom out of the business of telling fascinating tales about foreign lands. How it will be after the present war when you will tell your grandchildren that you have got to lunch with friends in London, but not to worry as you will be back for dinner and will bring them a box of butterscotch which you will pick up in Edinburgh on your way home—that is a prospect upon which I would much rather not dwell.

To me, the most fascinating passage in any travel book is that delightful sentence in Marco Polo's famous account of his voyage to China where he describes his party's arrival in the city of Bokhara and then casually remarks: "And here, from our inability to proceed further, we remained three years." Today the week-ender who misses the 8:00 from Old Greenwich (on account of that third cup of coffee which he really neither wanted nor needed) and has to wait for the 8:11 makes a great to-do about his discomforts, what with its being Monday morning and his desk still piled that high with Saturday's neglected correspondence. Wise Marco Millions found that he had to stay three years in the ancient Mohammedan stronghold. Did that fill his heart with despair? It did not. He learned something about the native vernacular, he explored the market place which was the center of the book trade for that part of the world, found out where you could eat the kush-kush (a local dish made out of lambs' eyes, cabbage, and garlic), made discreet inquiries until he had discovered which rich

Chapter III

merchant's daughter was not averse to the advances of a bright and good-looking Venetian lad, and undoubtedly had the time of his young life.

But that too belongs to another chapter, wherein I will tell you my observations upon our modern fallacy that travel is bound to broaden a person's outlook. For the moment, I have not yet proceeded any further than that curious museum in my native town where I made my first acquaintance with the earth and the wonders thereof. I think it was my grandfather who, not quite knowing what to do with me one bright Sunday morning, remembered that he was a charter member of this organization and that it would therefore not cost him anything if he took me there, whereas the other museum (that of the embalmed pictures) would charge him twenty-five cents admission. Grandpa was not the sort of person to pass up a chance like that. And so to the Willemskade we walked, and after the door had closed upon us and Grandpa had delivered his cane (all museums are very particular upon this subject: they seem to fear that the sight of so many glass cases will incite the visitors to acts of violent vandalism), I had the shock of my life, for I found myself face to face with a dark-skinned Laplander, hitching a full-sized (if slightly moth-eaten) reindeer to a sleigh which already contained his family, consisting of his wife and one child (of indefinable gender, it being so completely wrapped in furs that nothing showed but the eyes and 'part of the flat nose).

You will protest that I am indulging in a wild fantasy and cannot possibly remember all these details after more than half a century. To which I make reply that I am telling you the absolute truth. I shall experience a great many difficulties when, in the pursuit of certain autobiographical items, I finally reach the years immediately preceding the present one. If it were not for the fact that Jimmie has kept a line-a-day book ever since we were married, I would not know a thing about the last time we visited Lapland or on what ship we returned to America immediately before the outbreak of the present war. I once figured out that I had crossed the ocean fifty-seven times, but most of those voyages have become a complete hodgepodge of names and dates. On the other hand, I can give you an accurate description of the vessel on which I took my first river trip from Rotterdam to Dordrecht (when I was seven years old) and of what we had for dinner on my twelfth birthday, when I got an album of Moszkowski's *Spanish Dances* as my chief present. I remember the birthdays of my grandchildren because the beloved Janet, with a marvelous feeling for timing, bestowed them upon this world on the first, the second, and the third of November. But which particular one arrived on which particular date is a problem that has to be investigated every time that happy occasion comes along.

By the same token, I can still tell you the names and nicknames of all the boys in the group picture that was taken my first year at school, but I am apt to stare at a man (or what is much worse, a woman) with whom I had dinner a fortnight ago and swear that I have never seen the face until that moment. I have been told that this is a sure sign of oncoming age and that all older people suffer from the same uncomfortable mnemotechnic ailment. I shall let it go at that, but I assure you that every detail I give you about the first twenty years of my life is absolutely true. After that, I can be sure of a thing only if it has happened to find its way into my wife's daily diary.

Know ye therefore that it was this family of stuffed Laplanders plus reindeer that gave me my first desire to explore the whole of the world (as since then I have done pretty thoroughly), and that these same Laplanders induced me to investigate the rest of the museum, which in turn led to quite unexpected results. For this was long before the day of the scientific expert. The collection, therefore, had been gathered by well-meaning amateurs, few of whom had really known much about art but who had bought what they liked. As a result, it contained some terrible monstrosities, but it escaped that monotony of perfection which is the basis of many of our modern museums.

Then there was another circumstance which made for a greater diversity of interests than is to be found in our up-to-date accumulations of ancestral relics. The Kingdom of the Netherlands of half a century ago was class-ridden to an extent few members of the younger generation can any longer understand. Therefore, if one of the leading families of a town decided that the time had come to bestow a priceless heirloom upon the community at large, there was only one thing the director of the museum could do. I remember a case in point which took place not so many years ago. The members of one of the best local families had sent this unfortunate official a *pot de chambre* which was supposed to have been used by no one less than the great Napoleon when that mighty monarch had graced their ancestral premises for a single night during one of his rare visits to his Department of the Mouth of the Meuse, as Holland had been rebaptized when it had become a part of France. The director objected. The article in question was without any artistic value! If it had been of Sèvres or Wedgwood origin, he would gladly have exhibited it, but it was of a common ordinary variety and undoubtedly of domestic origin, for such pots could still be bought at any of the local stores for a couple of stivers. The family that owned this "night vase" (as the polite Dutch of another generation called a chamber pot) insisted. The vessel was sacrosanct, as no one else than the great Napoleon, etc., and they argued their point with the eloquence and fury of a Nazi who has got hold of the Führer's toothbrush and wants it exhibited in the china collection of the palace of Sans Souci. And so for several years the pot was alternately in and out of one of the showcases until the director hit upon the only possible solution and hired the cleaning woman to drop the thing, and in such a drastic manner that it could never possibly be repaired.

In some such manner my beloved museum must also have got hold of a couple of very inferior mummies which for some mysterious reason one of the leading shipowners of our port had once upon a time picked up in Paris. They were very raggy-looking and undoubtedly contained the mortal remains of very ordinary people—perhaps those of Moses' baker and his wife. But they were guaranteed to be thousands of years old, and I was fascinated by the thought that, if some miracle should suddenly bring them back to life, I would not have the slightest idea what to say to them, as they, of course, could speak only Egyptian and I knew nothing but Dutch. Furthermore, there was something gruesome about their set smiles, and all children love the macabre. And then, to have been dead for forty or fifty centuries and still to be an object of interest to onlookers was quite an achievement.

All I knew about death was the occasional disappearance of some superannuated fifth cousin, and she was usually forgotten before the rest of the family returned from the cemetery. Here, therefore, was a link with a past that extended for thousands of years beyond all those things that had happened in the cellar of the House of a Thousand Fears and in the East Gate when the faithful blacksmith had cleft the heads of half a hundred Spanish hirelings.

But one day, in a remote corner of one of the rooms, I discovered something which, according to the label on the case, made these Egyptian mummies look like veritable upstarts. The grinning skull inside, as I was able to spell out, had been dug up in the valley of one of the little tributaries of the Rhine, and it was that of a prehistoric man who might have lived as long as thirty thousand years ago. A few funny-looking bits of stone, reposing in a basket next to the skull, were said to have been part of the arms with which he had defended himself against the wild animals which then still inhabited the northern part of Europe. All this fitted in with an article on "Our Remote Ancestors" in a magazine which was the *St. Nicholas* of the Dutch children of the eighties.

That little monthly was to play quite a role in my life, but that did not happen until much later. I am not quite sure when I learned to read, but it must have been at a very early age, as I have always taken reading for granted. Now, it was during the late eighties that a couple of mastodons had been discovered in northern Siberia. Such discoveries were nothing new, but these two had been so well preserved by the glacier or the iceberg which had been responsible for their sudden death that they were as good as new, and their meat was so fresh that the dogs of the Russian expedition had literally torn them to pieces. My monthly had devoted quite a lot of space to this find on the ground that it showed God's hand; for by this means (of freezing the creatures in at that particular moment) He was able to show later generations just exactly what the world of 10,000 B.C. had looked like. The label placed near the skull in my museum drew no such moral lesson. It bluntly stated that the owner of this grim-looking cranium had probably lived some thirty thousand years before the beginning of the Christian era. He had therefore antedated the mastodons by almost twenty thousand years.

The questions I asked at home about this strange visitor to our gates were quickly side-stepped by my parents, who did not want to set up as experts on prehistory. They briefly told me to stick to my lessons and not to be so everlastingly curious about things that were no direct concern of mine, and I suppose that is what I did, for where could I have gone for further information? My school textbook did not take me further back than one hundred years B.C., when the first inhabitants—the fierce-looking Batavians—were said to have come sailing down to our marshes in rafts that had carried them down the Rhine. My ignorance about that skull therefore remained as complete as it had been before and as it has remained until this very day.

But, in spite of this, I must credit that ancient pate with having played quite a role in my life, for one day I suddenly asked myself the question, "What if it had been the head of one of my own ancestors?" The thing had been dug up not so far from where we lived, and it was perfectly possible, therefore, that it had belonged to one of my own great-great-great-great-grandfathers. Not that there was any striking family resemblance, for it looked exactly like the skull of the chimpanzee which was exhibited in the next case. But you never could tell, and it made life so much more interesting to imagine your ancestors fighting mastodons and tigers instead of going to dull offices as everybody I knew did every day of the year. Holidays were unknown, and it was the habit of every self-respecting businessman to pay at least one short visit to his counting-house on the Sabbath day to see what the Sunday mail had brought, for the postman also worked on the day of rest and continued to do so until a very recent date. Indeed, I still vividly remember our neighbor Belgium's great social step forward, when stamps were specially provided with a little perforated appendix informing the postal authorities that it was not necessary to deliver that particular letter on Sunday.

Like most children, I was thoroughly dissatisfied with my position in life and wondered why so charming and bright a lad as myself had been born into such a humdrum and commonplace family. My father attained his semiheroic proportions only on those rare occasions when he was obliged to leave his warm bed to venture forth into the cold of night and fight a fire. I had an uncle in the navy, but he belonged to the paymaster's department, and the medal he wore he had got for saving a child from drowning. For the rest, so far as I could see, there was nothing but dreary mediocrity, and a caveman ancestor was therefore a most welcome addition to that dream-like existence in which I spent so much of my time that at school I was always at the foot of my class. Incidentally, that evocative skull no longer exists. The Nazis settled its fate when they set fire to Rotterdam and, among a great many other things, destroyed my pet museum.

Time Out for a Short Breathing Space, During Which I Find Out Whether I Am Still on the Right Track

WHEN SAILING across a part of the map that he has never visited before, the careful mariner is ever busy studying the charts, examining the heavens, observing the tides and currents, and in every other way endeavoring to obtain whatever data are available to keep him on the right course. Today I am like those ancestors of ours who, armed only with a compass, a log, a sextant, and a few very beautifully engraved but (by our standards) hopelessly antiquated maps, set forth just the same to explore regions about which they knew nothing except what they had been able to learn from the toothless mariners who were swapping yarns in the taverns that lined the water front. My ultimate goal is some kind of autobiography that will tell only the little that is absolutely unavoidable about myself and as much as can possibly be crowded into seven hundred pages about those matters which have most of all interested me during my peregrinations through life.

In order to accomplish this dual purpose, I thought of a very simple device. I told Jimmie (who, as most people by now surely know, is my wife) to keep her blue pencil near at hand while copying this first draft. "You know," I reminded her, "I am a born wanderer. I have wandered all through life because I am so terribly curious about everything that goes on everywhere that I am forever getting off the main road to see what may be going on in some near-by field. A curious-looking church steeple will make me forget that we are bound for a luncheon date and that we ought to get there. A sort of finicky punctuality—a hangover from the days of my youth—and an intense dislike for being late have as a rule saved me from straying too far off the main track, but I know my weakness, especially when I am writing and am not working against a date line. So you go ahead and keep watch, and every time you notice that I have indulged a little too much in my beloved pastime, use your blue pencil and I will start all over again from the point where I strayed from the road."

Up to now, Jimmie has not been obliged to avail herself of her blue-penciling privilege, but I feel the mood coming on in me, for never has the temptation to stray been so great as in this case. And in order to save her the trouble, I have decided to pause a few moments and take stock of what I have done so far and what I mean to do from now on.

I found a tremendous satisfaction in writing about the days of my early youth. Now that the Germans have destroyed Rotterdam, Middelburg, and that part of The Hague with which I was most familiar, all those spots in which I had my roots are gone forever. Most of my relatives and a great many of my early friends are dead too, and I live in a sort of vacuum, as far as my own past is concerned. I shall never be able to return to a certain street along a certain canal in Rotterdam where I got so fascinated by the unloading of a cargo of pigs that I remained behind while my mother walked on alone, with the result that I became a "lost child" and, when recaptured, was severely punished because I "might have been stolen by the gypsies."

I shall never stand on the same rough cobblestones from where I watched my first Punch-and-Judy performance. Even the church in which I heard my first music no longer exists.

The Nazis burned everything to a flat uniformity, and the city that will arise from the ruins will bear no resemblance to the rabbit warren of crooked alleys and lanes which were the fascinating—if highly unhygienic—remnants of our medieval city and an everlasting source of wonder and delight to a small boy who suffered from an exaggerated sense of curiosity.

As for Middelburg, that perfect gem of a seventeenth-century Dutch city, the German shells did so much havoc that it can never be restored to its ancient charm. And The Hague, where the prophets of a New Era committed the sacrilege of filling up the municipal pond, which for almost seven centuries had been the citizens' pride and the center of Dutch national life —it undoubtedly will be rebuilt, but the woods in which I knew every tree are gone forever.

There is a terrific temptation to reconstruct these past scenes and to revive these bygone memories at the expense of everything else, and that, of course, is exactly what I must not do. So from time to time I shall stop long enough in my pleasant ramblings to see where I have got and to remind myself that I am writing for a somewhat larger public than the few survivors of that bygone era who share those memories with me. Such a moment, it seems to me, has now come, and I can think of no better way to fill this breathing space than by a short inquiry into the general subject of the art of writing autobiographies.

I had never given the matter much thought. I took it for granted that the old Greeks had given us that particular form of literary expression. Of course they had, for *autos* was Greek, and *bios* was Greek, and anyway, the Greeks had been the first to do everything (they had always "been there fustest" with the mostest brains, so to speak) and were the people who had invented—or foreshadowed, pioneered in, or improved upon— medicine, geometry, algebra, history, literature, the theater (both comedy and tragedy), music, the theorem of Pythagoras (if not up to 197 decimals), the theory of statecraft and the practice of democracy, Attic salt, the Olympic games, modern architecture, the college lecture system, women in politics, tyranny and demagogues, our alphabet, and olive oil for the complexion. Since they had done all those things (and a lot more of which I cannot think just now), I took it for granted that the first autobiography too had been the work of a Greek. But in this, as I have since discovered, I was entirely wrong. It takes a spiritual exhibitionist to write a good autobiography. Now, the ancient world had its share of physical exhibitionists and in the person of Alcibiades gave us an example that has rarely been surpassed. But I should have known enough not to look for the first true autobiographer among the Greeks, who were complete extroverts, who carried their hearts on their sleeves, and who kissed their girls right out on the steps of the Acropolis, whereas a successful autobiography can only be written by an introvert who lives molelike in the dark recesses of his own soul and who kisses his girl on the sly and then makes himself believe that he did it because it was good for her health. And it was not until a triumphant Christianity had done away with the old Greek philosophy of saying yea unto life and had introduced that new attitude towards life which growled a contemptuous no to all the claims of nature that there arose a type of man so thoroughly engrossed in his own inner life that he felt it to be his duty to share the tribulations of his immortal soul with his fellow citizens.

Since the early Christians, by force of circumstances, were forever under the obligation to bear public witness to their faith, they quite naturally developed an abnormal streak of that spiritual exhibitionism which was to make them so highly unpopular with their Greek and Roman neighbors. For the latter were not at all interested in the problematic pleasures of a life hereafter. Their heaven and hell, in so far as they existed at all, were nebulous regions where, at best, one was bored to death and upon which one wasted just as little thought as possible. And here these kitchen menials and scullery slaves and all these other humble little folk, who until then had never so much as dared to speak to their betters until first spoken to, now brazenly asked their masters whether they did not feel a deep anguish at the fate that awaited them, and then, for good measure, indulged in a hymn of praise which prevailed in their own souls, as if a respectable Roman matron or a superior Greek philosopher were subject to the same laws of divine retribution as the common rabble.

Our history books are very apt to explain the era of the great Christian persecutions as if they had been the result of the Roman hatred for the new god. I don't think that was it at all. Imperial Rome was so full of new gods that this new Jewish deity (as the contemporaries of Vespasian and Diocletian held him to be) attracted hardly any attention in his status as a god, and if his followers had contented themselves with quietly pursuing their own form of worship, nothing much would have happened to them. A few discreet bribes to the right police officers would have fixed that perplexing problem of paying a certain outward obeisance to the name of the Emperor, just as seventeen hundred years later, the Catholics of the Netherlands could maintain their own little chapels by occasionally dropping a couple of guilders into the outstretched palm of a precinct captain. And a divinity who had died on the cross was not likely to arouse a great deal of sympathy among the warlike Romans, who on occasions (for example, when they took some city that had indulged in piracy) would condemn thousands of their captives to this particular form of torture and death.

No, the Romans of the first century were about as much interested in the spiritual and theological aspects of that obscure new faith as the New Yorkers of 1944 are in the obscure doctrines preached every Sunday morning by some self-styled new prophet who hires the banqueting hall of a third-rate hotel to preach his homemade creed to those who are looking for still another short cut to salvation. What the civilized Romans of the beginning of our era resented in their Christian neighbors was their bad manners, not their belief in the god who had just been imported from the troublesome province of Palestine. Any too public demonstration of one's innermost feelings was bad manners in the eyes of the Romans, who in that respect were very much like our modern English.

What those who survived as late as the fourth century must therefore have thought of the first autobiography ever written by the hand of man we do not know, but we can easily guess. All the more so as the book bore the title of *Confessions,* and as confessions in the eyes of the aristocratic Romans were just as bad form as explanations or apologies. They probably consoled themselves with the thought that the author, although a Roman citizen by the name of Aurelius Augustinus, was a native of the African province of Numidia and therefore—to make the best of it—of suspiciously exotic origin. Certainly, a strange mingling of racial strains is strongly betrayed in the Oriental appetites of his youth. He lived a most worldly existence, and, though his mother was a Christian, the son was very far removed from sanctity until the inevitable day when sin suddenly palled upon him, and he repented of his ways and made a high resolve that from that moment on the ancient quarrel between the spirit and the flesh should be decided in favor of the former. If we are to believe the legend connected with the event, it was (among other things) the chance opening of a volume of the Epistles of Saint Paul which was responsible for this miracle. After that, there were to be no more rioting and drunkenness, no more chambering and wantonness, no more strife and envying, and no more provisioning for the lusts of the flesh. There was only to be the law of his Saviour.

On Easter of the year 387, Aurelius Augustinus received

holy baptism, and from that moment on until his death, more than half a century later, he labored diligently in the vineyard of the Lord. He was a most prolific writer, almost as rich in his literary output as Monsieur de Voltaire, with whom he shared that devotion to style which has given the works of these two authors their place of lasting pre-eminence among people of taste.

That quality—good writing—would not alone have accounted for the success of Saint Augustine. He also had something to say at a moment when the Church was going through the most serious crisis of its entire career. The time of persecutions had come to an end, and the era of the great internal convulsions had set in. It was impossible for anyone in the public eye not to take a definite stand in the quarrels that threatened to rend the Church asunder. It was not an easy position for a recent convert who, for the brilliancy of his mind and the vivid richness of his style, was by a great many people acclaimed a second Saint Paul. And since his early and far from exemplary existence was still clearly remembered by his contemporaries, Augustine felt the need of making his position as one of the mightiest champions of the new faith so definitely clear that no one could have any doubt about the absolute sincerity of his professions.

Hence his *Confessions* (written about the year 400), which was both an apology for his past and a program for the future of a world he hoped to see established on the basis of a truly Christian commonwealth.

That was an ideal he shared with many others. At the moment I am writing this, there are in America no fewer than two hundred and thirty-eight duly recognized organizations working for a new world of peace, justice, and righteousness which the members of these societies hope to establish upon the ruins of that older culture which is now rapidly tumbling to pieces. Saint Augustine had to wrestle with a problem that was exactly like our own. The Western Roman Empire had all but formally come to an end in the year 410, when Alaric, the King of the West Goths, had taken and sacked Rome and had bottled up the Roman emperors in their new capital of Ravenna. Saint Augustine, then fifty-six years old, had a clean slate upon which to write down his plans for the future. Being above all things a man of letters, he chose the confessional approach to give expression to his ideas. And in that way the world got its first true autobiography.

After that, almost twelve centuries had to go by before the reading public was once again offered a comparable chance to follow the spiritual vicissitudes of a man who had given up the ways of this world to devote himself entirely to the success of the Lord. I refer to a book now practically unknown (and heaven knows, it is hard reading), entitled *Grace Abounding*, by John Bunyan, the literary tinker and the famous author of *Pilgrim's Progress*.

In the meantime, however, it had been able to peruse a collection of self-confessions of a very different nature: the autobiography of Benvenuto Cellini. A first-rate sculptor and worker in precious metals, he also distinguished himself as a most quarrelsome character. Every time he was requested to come to some city to do a particular piece of work, his visit ended in a brawl, invariably accompanied by the violent death of a couple of citizens who had incurred his displeasure. He was absolutely unscrupulous in monetary affairs and on one occasion went so far as to embezzle the jewels of the Pope's tiara, temporarily entrusted to his care. His endless affairs with other people's wives also contributed to his reputation as a thoroughly bad performer, and that in an era—the Renaissance —when morals had become a memory.

What prompted this picaresque and colorful scoundrel to write his autobiography we do not know, but when he was almost sixty years old (in spite of the irregularities of his life he reached the ripe old age of seventy-one) he set himself down to tell posterity all about his adventures and his villainies. He was a man of inordinate vanity, as proud of the way he had slain his brother's murderer as he was of the wiles by which he had betrayed some unsuspecting woman, and he spared us no details when it came to acts of perfidy that normal people would have hidden at all cost.

Indeed, there is only one other out-and-out autobiography which rivals Cellini's in the brazen honesty with which we are informed about its hero's transgressions against his fellow men and women. These are the well-known memoirs of that magnificent fraud who called himself Count Casanova. During the seventy-three restless years he spent on this earth, he visited almost every court of Europe and was banished from practically every country and town. But being a fellow of parts, he somehow extricated himself successfully from every unfortunate impasse and even fled from the terrible state prison of Venice, from which nobody else either before or afterwards was ever able to escape. And he died most respectably, as the librarian of Count Waldstein, at that gentleman's castle of Dux, in Bohemia. During his retirement in that remote place he composed the many volumes of his memorable memoirs. A complete cynic, like Cellini, he spared himself in no possible way, but being a trained writer (which Cellini had not been), he gave us a work of genuine historical importance. Wherever we are able to check him, we find (rather to our surprise) that he stuck pretty closely to the truth. Only where he kisses and tells do we discover that he sometimes felt inclined to tell without having done any kissing. And, of course, it is the amorous part of his literary legacy that has always attracted the attention of the majority of his readers and which has placed his memoirs among the few perennial autobiographies that were to become models for all subsequent efforts in the confidential form of literature.

Chapter IV

In the month of June of the year 1712, one Isaac Rousseau, an honorable watchmaker of the Republic of Geneva (today it is still the only canton of Switzerland which proudly proclaims itself a republic), became the father of a sickly child who was given the name of Jean-Jacques. Our world of today would look very different from what it does if this event had never taken place. For little Jean-Jacques survived the many maladies of his childhood days to become the successful publicist of that new Age of Reason which based its hopes for the future upon the triumph of human reason and which plunged Europe into that blood-smeared revolutionary era which finally led to the tyranny of Napoleon and the reactionary period of Metternich.

He was neither a religious zealot, as Saint Augustine and John Bunyan had been before him, nor an adventurer in the grand style of Cellini and Casanova. But he surpassed all four of them as an exhibitionist, and when he started out to show us a man in all the truth of nature (as he did in the *Confessions* he wrote between the years 1781 and 1788), he fully lived up to his promise. By the time we reach the last page of this dreary opus (which few people during our own generation have been able to pursue to the end) we know all about him—indeed we know so much about him that we come to dislike him most cordially; for, though the perfect egotist, he lacks every vestige of those colorful qualities which are the main attraction of the works of Cellini and Casanova. He remains throughout a little middle-class Swiss boy, with all the Calvinistic inhibitions of his early training, and in the presence of his betters he can never forget that he started life as a lackey.

I believe that modern science calls the kind of autobiography written according to the Rousseau pattern (and almost all modern autobiographies have heavily leaned upon Rousseau's *Confessions*) "psychological." I know that doctors, when they cannot quite diagnose a patient's ailments, tell him that

79

it is probably a case of nerves. By the same token, the word psychology has come to cover a mass of bad taste, and in no other field has it done quite so much harm as in literature.

Politically, Rousseau's writings about the perfection of original man (about whom he knew absolutely nothing) and his subsequent fall from grace when he became exposed to civilization caused an enormous amount of confusion, comparable only to the havoc which, a century and a half later, was wrought by Hitler's and Rosenberg's nonsense about the virtues of their nonexisting Aryan race. But the society in which Rousseau lived had long since outlived its own usefulness, and it would have come to an end anyway, regardless of Jean-Jacques' sentimental prattling. It was the shameless self-exposé of this wretched little copyist, wandering secretary, servant-girl chaser, and exploiter of credulous old women that made his influence so dangerous for the future. Ever since, the shallow and cheap minds, which if left to their own devices would never have dared to do so, have favored us with their ineffectual love affairs and their perambulations through the dull and monotonous fields of illicit amatory practice as if they had been so many Tristans and Isoldes, and as if it really greatly mattered whether a fellow with the soul of a shipping clerk felt a temporary yen for a commonplace little girl who worked in the invoice department. Love is a delicate matter, which should be approached either with the deft hand of a Hofmannsthal or the delicate touch of a Dante, who in a single sentence about his Paolo and Francesca ("the book slipped out of our hands, and that night we read no further" *) is able to tell you more about what happened to them than you can derive from a dozen pages of the applied physiology of D. H. Lawrence.

---

* A far from accurate but psychologically true rendering of *Inferno,* V, 138.—Ed.

Chapter IV

Feeling the way I do about that sort of autobiography, I am not exactly an ideal candidate for self-confessional honors. I would as soon reveal such intimate details about my own past as I would volunteer to undress in one of Macy's shopwindows. Of course, I know that very useful autobiographies have been written by great statesmen, famous authors, distinguished scientists, successful and unsuccessful revolutionists, spook doctors, musicians, and other kinds of citizens, but some of them had actually played a prominent role in the historical development of their own day, while others at least thought that they had done so, or wished to prove a point which had escaped their contemporaries and which—although posthumously—they meant to bring to their attention. Moreover, most of these wrote memoirs rather than regular autobiographies.

But what should I be able to say about myself? I have never played any kind of role in politics. The farthest I got was a few years ago, when I was offered the Democratic candidacy for Congress for our district in the sovereign state of Connecticut. But I preferred to leave the field to Clare Luce, for I was sure that she would enjoy the experience much more than I. I had never met the lady, but on hearsay evidence I considered her ideally suited for that kind of work, and she has indeed done everything we expected of her.

Neither had I distinguished myself during my days as a war correspondent sufficiently to feel that the world would want to know more about my adventures. In short, my life, as I look back upon it, has been so completely devoid of anything of cosmic importance that the whole story could be easily retold in fifteen lines in *Who's Who*.

But while studying the problem of autobiography, about which there is not very much to be found in our handbooks of literature, I came to think of another type of self-confessional book which had always interested me much more than the regular autobiographies. I refer to the works of a number of people of a meditative turn of mind who wrote about almost anything under the sun but who somehow mingled their own personality with their observations upon whatever subject they chose to discuss. It is difficult to bring these authors together in a definite category, but none of them, no matter when they lived or what problems of life they took for their particular topics (fishing, exploring, spending seventy years in a monastery, going to war, or agitating for peace everlasting), could help but reveal at least part of their own selves in the subject under discussion. And if that self happened to be the reflection of a man or woman of charm or intelligence or wisdom (or all three combined), the result was invariably a most delightful experience to the reader who had eyes with which to see the unwritten word and ears with which to hear the whispered sentence.

No one, of course, was such a past master at that subtle art of the indirect revelation as my beloved old friend, the Sieur de Montaigne. For when you have read his *Essays,* you know him as if you had spent half your life at the castle from which the Eyquem family (after it had come to affluence and honor) had borrowed its title.

Then there were the *Gedanken und Erinnerungen* of Goethe. I am not very fond of the Minister of State of the Grand Duchy of Weimar. I infinitely prefer the retired herring merchant and honorary citizen of the town of Rome, who was a hundred per cent more human than the grand-ducal official. Goethe would have made an ideal president of Harvard. But God knows he could write, and when he got really going and was at his best (*Über allen Gipfeln ist Ruh*) there has been nobody to surpass him. He spent all his life in cellophane, and he was most careful to have his hair neatly powdered and his clothes well brushed before he showed himself to the populace. Indeed, he was the sort of person to wear his grand cross of the Order of the Lippe-Detmold Eagle on his nightshirt, and

Chapter IV

he would have been about the last person Frits and I would have dreamed of inviting to our Veere dinner parties. Just the same, his *Dichtung und Wahrheit* (a title for which I have never yet found an adequate translation) gives such a clear picture of the kind of people who lived during the latter half of the eighteenth century (the author himself included) that those contemplating the self-revelatory crime of an autobiography should try and read at least through the first half. It is not so dull as Marx's opus on capital (which I think holds the all-high prize for unreadability, together with a number of religious books, such as the Koran, the *Book of Mormon,* and Mother Eddy's *Science and Health*), but it takes an effort to follow the *Herr Geheimrat,* and I have a suspicion that his prolonged absences from his mother (for which he invariably got the blame) may have been due in the first instance to Mamma's fear of having to put up for more than a few days with that son who probably came down to breakfast in the full-dress uniform of a member of the grand-ducal council of state.

"Yes," I can hear her say, "my son has gone pretty far in this world, and I am very proud of him, but I wish he could ask me to pass him the jam without worrying about how Terence would have put the sentence into iambics." For Mamma Goethe dearly loved her puns, for which I bless her. The two best friends I ever had—my wife Jimmie and Ben Huebsch the publisher—were addicted to this amiable weakness. All the other guests might leave the table, but I stayed on, with the greedy look of my blessed grandchildren when Elsie has whispered into their ears that there is still a third portion of ice cream left in the pantry.

Do I know of still other books of this kind which pretend to discuss all sorts of innocuous subjects and which are really autobiography in disguise? Yes, I know of quite a few, but, in the first place, the war bids me be brief (no paper for purely literary purposes) and, in the second place, they are not the kinds of books that get easily translated, and I have never liked those people who tell me, "Ah, but you should have read that little morsel from the Upanishads in the original Sanskrit."

According to the professors, there are about fifteen hundred different languages in this world. I have learned to grope my way through about a dozen, and that is enough for one lifetime.

Here I got a note from my wife, busy copying my hieroglyphics in the other room. "Come back home, 'Enery," it read. "You are wandering a little too much." When I hear the voice of authority speaking with that particular emphasis, I usually find it wise to obey and so I shall now treat you to a short summing-up of my plans.

I shall, as the preacher said, endeavor to walk the narrow path between the right and wrong. Expect neither Saint Augustine nor Jean-Jacques Rousseau, but be prepared to come across a considerable amount of Montaigne, for he has been my steady companion for so many years that I could not now shake him, even if I tried. For the rest, I shall lay down no definite program, since I have already discovered that this is going to be one of those books that write themselves, with nothing to be done about it. Once you are in the saddle of such an unruly quadruped, you either go whither it takes you or give up the ride altogether. In this case I shall, of course, try to keep some kind of hold on the reins so as to keep the animal from indulging in a wild plunge that may make both of us break our necks. And when the wild ride has come to an end, I shall go through the manuscript with a blue pencil in my hand and a copy before me of a letter sent me by a remote friend after he heard that I had started work on what the newspapers had announced as my autobiography. "Remember," he said, "that there are certain things you cannot write about, no matter how good they are, especially when they touch upon the lives of women and children who are part of your own existence."

I appreciated his advice, but he could have saved himself the trouble, for that was exactly what I had intended to do. The things I have thought belong to the world in general, but the life I have lived is the private property of myself and of those who have shared my adventures with me. I am sure that Saint Peter will approve.

The other day I got hold of one of those statistical reports that are issued at irregular intervals by the Celestial Publicity Office. I looked down the list that gave the occupations of all the successful candidates of the last twenty years. When I came to the division of "columnists" I found a blank. None had been admitted.

CHAPTER V

As I Should Rather Like to Know What Made Me What I Am Today, I Do a Little Inquiring Into What Made My Ancestors What They Were in Their Own Day and Age

THE HISTORY of every nation begins with a myth. No matter in what remote corner of the earth we have dug into the past of people just discovered, we have invariably found ourselves lost among a weird tangle of fairy stories, all of which have one thing in common. They try to give some vague tradition a greater value and more prestige by tracing it back to a supernatural source.

Since nations are surprisingly like ordinary human beings and seem to grow up and develop according to a similar pattern (and to grow old and die, too, the same way), this is only natural. What makes it amusing is the fact that all of us can study this phenomenon in the laboratory of our own experience. Even today, millions of people flatly refuse to accept the story of creation presented to them as the approximate truth by the followers of the late Charles Darwin. They hate the idea so thoroughly and reject it so bitterly that in certain parts of the hinterland it may greatly interfere with your life if you so much as reveal your suspicions about the truth of Genesis 1.

I remember some twenty-five years ago, when I went to teach

in one of our small Midwestern colleges, how my first visit
was to the local butcher store to get some meat for the cat. The
woman who sold me the meat looked at me suspiciously and
said, "You are the new history professor, ain't you? Well, I
hope you're not going to teach our children that nonsense
about monkeys being their grandfathers."

I promised her I should be careful not to, provided she
would not sell me monkey meat for beef, and that was that.
But things do not seem to have changed very much, for only
five years ago and from the same region, which is alternately
known as the Bible or the Goiter Belt, I received a succession of
scurrilous letters from a clergyman who was apparently engaged in saving the faithful from the aftereffects of Robert
Ingersoll's crusade for reason. The fellow harped upon one
statement in my *Story of Mankind* in which I rather remotely
alluded to the theories of Charles Darwin. After a while I got
tired of the man's offensive letters, and when he became in-
sistent that we debate the subject in the largest hall in Ohio
(charging admission and splitting the money three ways—one
third to him, one third to me, and one third to the promoter),
I sent him a telegram, signed Charles Darwin, informing him
that my good friend, Dr. van Loon, had showed me his chal-
lenge and that I was willing to accept it and would come to
Ohio at the first possible opportunity, provided he gave the
name Darwin as much publicity as his own. He fell for the
bait and, telegraphing his reply to Professor Charles Darwin,
expressed his delight that at last he could come to grips with
the inventor of that infamous lie which cast a shadow upon
the divine origin of man. He informed me that the stage was
set for our debate.

He was apparently unaware of the fact that the eminent
biologist had died the same year I was born. But then, there
was a lot he had not yet learned.

By mere chance, a few years later, I read a little item in a newspaper that the fellow's daughter, trying to escape from the parental roof, had reached out for the branch of a tree outside her window and that she had fallen and had been seriously injured. I felt sorry. Her nonsimian ancestry had apparently worked against her.

It is, of course, very easy to be funny about these poor deluded creatures who stick for years and often for centuries to absurd beliefs that science has long since proved to be entirely erroneous. But the average of the human race being what it is and the lethargy of the average human mind being infinitely worse than that of the sloth (*Bradypus torporensis*), who is said to be unwilling to move even if a fire is lighted right underneath him, we can hardly expect otherwise. In addition to which, there is the matter of pride. The acquisition of a fact, no matter how simple or self-evident, is a considerable problem to that "common man" who recently has been proclaimed the beginning and the end of all wisdom. When at the age of twelve he has finally accepted the axiom that parallel lines can never meet, he is not going to take it lying down when some German professor comes along and proves to him that they do. Since he is unable to refute Mr. Einstein on his own ground, he will draw attention to his long hair or call him a Jew (which is even easier), and it may take centuries before his great-grandchildren at last surrender and allow themselves to be convinced.

When a historian tries to persuade him that there is nothing "definite" about the famous date of July 4, 1776, because in another ten thousand years or so, when our calendar will be once more out of gear, that date may have to be shoved a few days forward, he will denounce the poor man as one lacking in patriotic ardor and will loudly holler for the Honorable Martin Dies to come and arrest the dirty Communist. And if he had his way, he would have every book upon the subject of non-Euclidian geometry burned, even as the Nazis have burned mine. For to him the names of Gans, Lobachevski, Bolyai, and Riemann are as abhorrent as those of Luther and Calvin and Zwingli were to the Catholic authorities of the sixteenth century. If the faithful were allowed to express doubt in any way connected with the very foundations of the Faith as it had been accepted for fifteen centuries, and were permitted to have even a fraction of their skepticism unchallenged, the whole fabric of the Church would be exposed to collapse, just as a slight crack at the bottom of a mighty tower may cause it to fall.

I was, of course, indulging in a harmless *Spielerei* when I gave those examples of the parallel lines and the Fourth of July. Even the great pioneers of the non-Euclidian geometry agreed that the geometry of small spaces will always remain approximately Euclidian; few people are ever faced with the problem of baking a birthday cake with a diameter of a billion miles, and none will be asked to say a few words at the Independence Day celebrations of the year 11,943. But there are certain questions which deeply affect the convictions of the average sane and sound citizen, and when someone dares touch one of those, which are part of his prejudices and therefore sacred, then there is likely to be trouble, and heads are likely to fall.

During the last five hundred years the human race has experienced three terrific blows in its solar plexus, from several of which it has not yet recovered. The first one took place at about the same time America was discovered. It did away with the flattering conception that this earth was the center of the universe. It was proved to be not even the center of our own planetary system and was reduced to the rank of an inconsequential speck of dust in a nineteenth-rate constellation, way out somewhere in the suburbs of God's mighty firmament. This assertion caused such an outbreak of indignation that quite a number of people lost their lives in the subsequent scuffle, and others escaped a similar fate only by a last-moment retraction. But even today, and within the very shadow of a city like Chicago, there are thousands of people who reject this hypothesis with the violence of a Christian Science healer brought face to face with the microbes responsible for giving him a nice case of dysentery.

When finally the last smoke of the last funeral pyre had cleared away (for good and all, let us hope), there were signs that another terrific blow was about to be administered. When it came, it caused a violent commotion, for it denied man's divine origin and made him a brother of the animals of the field. As Darwin had published his final proof of something that had been suspected ever since the days of the Middle Ages (Roger Bacon, who died in 1294, already seems to have played with the idea) in the year 1859 and in his subsequent *Descent of Man* (1871), the debate was still in full swing when I made my appearance in this world. But since I was born into a family that was completely Voltairian in its views and had relegated religion to the kitchen, I was completely unconscious of the reverberations it had caused until after I had come to America and found to my great surprise that it was still an issue which was able to make otherwise harmless people rise in profound wrath and even commit mayhem upon anyone rash enough to accuse them of being descended from monkeys. And though in the *Story of Mankind* I hardly touched upon the subject, hardly a week goes by (even now, more than twenty years after it appeared) without my receiving a letter calling me a diversity of vile names on account of my loose Darwinian morals. Furthermore, that rather primitive and entirely harmless book has been forbidden in the school libraries of more than a dozen states, and when I was in Baltimore working for the good old *Sun,* the city librarian of that noble stronghold of Southern gentility successfully kept *Mankind* off his shelves.

Chapter V

The third blow was administered when I was in my twenties, and the pugilist in this case was a mild Viennese professor by the name of Sigmund Freud. It is still too soon to sum up in a single sentence what he actually accomplished by his psychological discoveries, and besides I am too hopelessly ignorant of the subject to tell you anything of the slightest value. But I think that someday the name of Sigmund Freud will be placed in mankind's Hall of Fame, together with those of Copernicus, Galileo, and Darwin. For he cured the human race of the obsession that the soul was something like the captain of a ship and the undisputed master of man's fate. He showed us that there are other directing agencies which work in the dark obscurity of the hold, never come near the bridge, and are never allowed on deck (where they would cause a terrific commotion among the respectable passengers), but which nevertheless exist and play a leading role in deciding the course the vessel is to follow.

I have by the simple process of direct inquiry discovered that almost every person I meet is just as touchy as I am when it comes to the memories of his own earliest childhood days. I have also found that these memories can be divided into definite categories. Some people firmly maintain that they could read their Bible at the age of three and could write a passable letter at the age of four. There are large numbers who were able to play difficult musical compositions before they had ever learned their letters or their notes. There are those who distinctly remember fires which, according to our chronologies, took place a number of years before they were born. There are others who have vivid recollections of houses (usually Grandpa's farm, where they were allowed to ride Janey, the old mare), although these houses, according to Grandpappy's own testimony, had been torn down to the ground before his daughter had even been married and had only survived in a badly faded photograph in the family parlor.

Now, in view of the solemn attestations of these cheerful liars, I feel exceedingly uncomfortable when I in turn have to tell you about my earliest recollections. How far do they bear any resemblance to the actual truth, and to what extent are they the result of something somebody told me years afterwards and which I have so thoroughly incorporated into my own mental scrapbook that I have since come to accept them as the gospel truth? I have most carefully gone over the records, and I now beg to offer the following highly important items as the earliest data I can definitely connect with my terrestrial existence.

I was four years old, and the house was being whitewashed, one of the semiannually returning tortures of what, in the Holland of my day, was known as the "Great Housecleaning." It was Sunday afternoon, and I was playing in the kitchen—a privilege accorded me only on that holy day. I have already told you that the cellars underneath our house were part of the monastery which had stood on that spot several centuries before, and how I feared those sepulchral cavities. But now they were filled with the paraphernalia of painters and whitewashers, and I hoped to find a piece of putty with which to exercise my abilities as a sculptor. (When one is four years old, there are all sorts of wondrous things one can do with a piece of putty.) Taking putty, of course, was stealing, but, since I had not enjoyed the blessings of any kind of Christian bringing-up, the Eighth Commandment did not loom very large in my consciousness. I found my putty—a large lump of it, the biggest one I had ever had—and full of anticipatory delight, I sat down on what I thought was a small bench, to make a nose, the facial characteristic with which most children seem to start their experiments in portraiture.

But alas, the bench was no bench, but a small vat of whitewash, covered with a drab piece of cloth. And I splashed right into the cold and cloying liquid.

Chapter V

I was at that moment wearing a red dress with white lace trimming, for in those days little boys were kept in girls' clothes much longer than they are today, when two-year-olds may already be seen sporting regular pantaloons. I was, of course, immediately rescued by the maids, but the dress was spoiled beyond the hope of repair, and after that I was allowed to wear grown-up clothes. That is probably why I remember the event, for it freed me from the humiliating bondage of girlhood.

Recollection Number Two. It was my father's birthday, the twentieth of March, a great day in the lives of my sister and myself because we had all the pastry we wanted. Birthdays in Holland were important events, and in the afternoon it was open house for friends and relatives. Many of those relatives were merely family retainers, and one had to go back to the days of Caesar to find a common ancestor. But free cake and free port and sherry were something not to be overlooked by rather hungry old ladies and gentlemen, some of whom, alas! had seen much, much better days.

Among the latter there was a cousin who fascinated me because he wore a wig. It was a little brown wig and it was not very well made. Rumor has it that when I was still in my swaddling clothes, my aunts, who were then gay young women, tried to bribe me with the promise of a spoonful of brown sugar (molasses, as we call it over here) to pull the old gentleman's wig off, but I can't remember ever having been conscious of such an offer. Besides, I was much too scared of this strange creature, who for all the world looked like the sort of person Hogarth loved to draw. I am under the impression that he was even older than he looked, and he may well have been one of my many direct links with the eighteenth century.

On this particular day, the dear cousin was of course in evidence, and I came upon him in a corner of the room at the very moment when he was inserting an entire piece of pastry into his mouth. I have never forgotten that piece of pastry. It had a brown, nutty crust and must have had a diameter of from three to four inches. But he put the whole contraption into his mouth, and then closed his jaws and bent down to kiss me. I shrieked in horror and fled to the arms of my sister, who, being six years older than I, was the natural buffer between myself and the less pleasant aspects of life. My wicked behavior was speedily explained away with a reference to the excitement such a small boy must feel when surrounded by so many grown-ups. But the incident somehow stuck.

A few days ago, when I had started work on this chapter and happened to have dinner at the Lafayette with George Horowitz, I told him of my aged cousin's accomplishment, and he (being of a contrary sort of mind, for which reason I love him) said there was nothing to it. Anybody could do it. I bet him the price of the meal if either of us was able to repeat this feat. And so we ordered a whole tray of French pastry, with Gracie * to judge the contest. We both did our best, but neither of us succeeded, and we had to call it a draw. The unknown cousin therefore continues to hold the record. Maybe I have unconsciously come to associate him with the English cartoons of the beginning of the last century, showing Napoleon swallowing whole empires, but that he, on that occasion, gulped down an entire *taartje* (O blessed word of Holland's juvenile glossary) is a fact to which I will swear before two dozen notaries public. I mention it because it shows that absurd trivialities will stick in our memories while we are apt to forget events of genuine importance.

Recollection Number Three. I was taken in the train to The Hague, and from there I went by horsecar to Scheveningen. The week before, the Kurhaus, the largest hotel on the seashore, had burned down. The fire had been due to the care-

---

* Grace Castagnetta.

I behold my first great catastrophe.

lessness of a maid who had been heating her mistress's
curling iron too close to a lace curtain. That ominous detail
was duly impressed upon all the young women in our party,
and it made about as much impression as a warning to the present generation about smoking in bed and setting fire to the
sheets.

The memory I retain of my visit to the place of disaster is so
fresh and so clear that I can draw the scene in all its details, although it must have been more than half a century ago that
it happened. It may have been the suddenness with which we
came upon the charred ruins. The fire had done its job most
efficiently. Nothing remained except the blackened walls and
the gaping windows. Years afterwards I was to see an endless
number of just such silhouettes, but none of them gave me
such a clear feeling of the relentless cruelty of nature's blind
violence as this gray pile of stones. I also remember the occasion because it was the first time I was big enough to eat in a
restaurant. The meal has now escaped me, but what took my
special attention was the thickness of the cups and plates. In
those days, china was much more brittle than it is today, and
the restaurant keepers, in order not to go bankrupt through
breakage, had to provide themselves with tableware that
weighed a ton.

And now I come to Recollection Number Four, which (according to our modern psychologists) should have absolutely
conditioned the rest of my life, except that at that moment I
had not the slightest idea what it was all about. I told you
that every day, if the weather was at all tolerable (which only
too often it was not in our North Sea marshes), my mother
would take me for a walk. One afternoon she conducted me
(rather solemnly, it seemed to me) to a street through which
ran a railroad viaduct connecting the southern part of Holland
with the northern. I noticed a number of people standing underneath the viaduct and staring up at a rather obscure house

almost completely hidden by the larger ones on both sides. All the windows of that drab dwelling had been smashed. The blinds were hanging crazily from their hinges, and the door had apparently been broken in by some heavy blows of a hammer, as it was badly splintered and the lock was gone.

Since I had lived all my life in a community where law and order were observed so punctiliously that a murder occurred only about once a year, the sight of this wanton violence filled my young heart with a horror I find it very difficult to recapture. With our entire planet turned into a shambles, a few smashed windows are nothing to get excited about, but half a century ago such a waste of good plate glass was something unheard of.

"What happened?" I asked my mother, tightly clutching her gloved hand. I loved the touch of the warm, soft leather, but on that occasion I wanted protection against some unseen force of evil.

"There were Socialists hidden in that house," she whispered back, "and last night the people drove them out."

I had no idea what Socialists were, but I was sure they were something terrible. That impression stayed with me for a very long time, and it was not until much later that I began to get a clearer view of the subject. I then discovered that at about the time I was born there had been a whole series of outbreaks of labor discontent and that Rotterdam had been the center of a great many of them. I now know that labor conditions in the Netherlands of the eighties (as everywhere else) were a public scandal. But in our Calvinistic community the poor were merely something we would always have with us, and, since they were part of the ordained state of society, there was nothing much anybody would ever be able to do about them except by means of private charity, soup kitchens, homes for the homeless (and what homes!), and seats in the rear part of

At the age of six I came for the first time in contact with
"applied sociology."

the churches, where their presence would be neither observed
nor smelled.

Now when Socialism started upon its somewhat precarious
career during the middle of the last century, it was, of course,
regarded at first as a most dangerous menace to the existing
order of things. It is rather difficult today, when practically
every country in Europe before the advent of Hitler was dominated by Socialists, when kings and queens would have amiable social intercourse with their Socialist prime ministers
(and get beaten by them at bridge), to imagine a time when
the mere mention of the word "Socialist" would throw otherwise perfectly intelligent and well-balanced people into parox-
ysms of fear. Even our own Red scare of a few years ago, before
the Bolsheviks became our valued allies, was as nothing compared with the hatred and abhorrence all respectable citizens
then felt towards the followers of Marx and Engels. For the
throne and the altar (and regular and safe dividends) were
still the pillars upon which the fabric of state rested, and it
was a well-known fact that the Socialists wanted to take away
everybody's wealth, throw it into a large bin, and then divide
it equally among all the people so that everybody would be
equally rich. "And what will happen then?" the blessed who
have would ask each other with great conviction, aware of
being about to utter a profound verity. "The industrious ones
will go to work and soon they will again accumulate the fruit
of their labors, while these lazy bums [the Socialists] will live
high, wide, and handsome for a short space of time, and then
they will be even poorer than they were before. For that is the
way it always has been and always will be, world without end
—and what are American railroad shares and Sumatra tobacco
doing today?"

This nonsense was still being repeated twenty years later,
and all-the-money-in-a-pot-and-then-divide-it was to the Socialist cause of the eighties and nineties what the absurd yarn

about the nationalization of women meant to the Communist problem of 1918. Even today one will still occasionally meet it in some remote corner of the Hillbilly Alps or Park Avenue, and, though the literature upon Socialism would now fill a couple of Yankee Stadiums, ignorance of the true nature of the doctrines of the late Dr. Karl Marx still remains as profound as it was at the time when the good doctor had to eke out a living as London correspondent of the *New York Tribune*. And, although the Russian laws concerning divorce are much more stringent than our own, women in the Union of Soviet Socialist Republics will (for us) continue to be "nationalized": for error is as tough as poison ivy, and no one thus far has devised a way of getting rid of it.

Yes, in that curious manner I was for the first time in my life brought in contact with applied sociology. I came home an ardent royalist, and for quite a while I refrained from drawing extra whiskers (God knows, he had enough!) on the pictures of His Majesty which adorned the covers of our copybooks. I also chimed in right lustily when we little boys intoned our hymn of hate for all Socialists, a song I still remember.

One of the early leaders of the movement in the Netherlands was a certain Domela Nieuwenhuis. He was a man of high ethical principles and, if I am not mistaken, an ex-minister. But like his contemporary, poor Vincent van Gogh, he had been so deeply hurt by what he had seen in the slums of our big cities that he had decided to devote himself to the cause of the underprivileged. He seems to have been a completely harmless creature. In spite of his awe-inspiring appearance, he was the incarnation of mildness, but when a scapegoat was needed for these first clashes between striking laborers and the police, he was it. He was duly apprehended and condemned to a short term in prison.

In those days it was very difficult (as it still is even now) to find the right kind of occupation for the inmates of our penal

Those covers helped us get through the dullest parts of our lessons. We improved upon the royal physiognomies.

We then gave up changing those illustrious faces but de-voted our attention to the lower extremities, and the House of Orange went in for pipe smoking in a heavy way.

institutions, for of course they must under no circumstances be allowed to compete with the free labor outside. Most of them therefore had to make paper bags. The idea of a gentleman making paper bags (for D.N. belonged by birth to the so-called "upper classes") struck us kids as hilariously funny. No sooner had he been put behind the bars than all of us were repeating the brilliant refrain:

> *Nieuwenhuis is packing bags.*
> *Hee-ha-ho!*
> *Nieuwenhuis is packing bags.*
> *Hee-ha-ho!*

and so on, *ad infinitum* and *ad nauseam.*

Just before the war (but I am depending upon a memory that is not very good for the more recent events) Domela Nieuwenhuis was honored with a simple monument in the good city of Amsterdam. And today he is considered about as much of a revolutionist as John Adams, and much less than Tom Paine.

Another souvenir of those days of commotion has somehow clung to me. Either just before or after the appearance of the good Nieuwenhuis, another wicked agitator made his appearance in my native city. His name was de Vletter, and by profession he was a schoolteacher. One evening a crowd of his followers, exasperated at the illegal arrest of some of their comrades (the constitution did not carry much weight when the city fathers decided to break up a Socialist meeting), did a very foolish thing. They attacked the old town hall (since destroyed by the Nazis) and set the prisoners free. This led to a most regrettable outbreak of violence, and for a short while it looked as if (as the contemporary papers expressed themselves) our fair town would be subjected to a regular Reign of Terror, according to the best precedents of the French Revolution. All respectable citizens were sworn in as auxiliary policemen. My father was one of them, and he was armed with a derringer to protect life and limb. It is not known that he ever had the opportunity to use this instrument of destruction, but in my eyes the very possession of such an implement of war made him a hero, quite as much as did his badge and staff as an officer of one of our local fire companies. I always wanted to have that derringer and finally I got it. Curious to reflect, I do not own a single other personal souvenir of the author of my being. Whatever was put into a storehouse after his death was destroyed when the Nazis turned Rotterdam into a fiery beacon of warning to all the other small nations of Europe. This little derringer alone survived. At this very moment it is before me on my desk. It makes a handy paperweight.

And now to Early Recollection Number Five, of a much happier nature. My mother, as usual, had taken me out for my daily airing. It was rather late when we were returning from the harbor towards which I had dragged her to indulge in my pet hobby of seeing the pigs being loaded into the provincial river boats. In those days, the poor porkers were hoisted on board by the simple device of putting a loop around one of their hind legs and then, upsydaisy! they were on deck in no time. I suppose it made a rather uncomfortable method of transportation, but it was very funny to see them floating through the air and squealing their heads off in the way only a pig can squeal when he objects to the treatment he is receiving at human hands.

On our way home, my mother took the road that led by the old church of St. Lawrence (since then destroyed by the Germans). The front door, which was always closed except on Sunday mornings, stood wide open. We entered, and for the first time in my life I was inside a church. There were lots of people sitting in the pews, and a great many others were stand-

To be taken for a walk and shown the busy port was the greatest treat of all.

ing. There was no sermon being preached: the pulpit was empty, but the edifice was filled with the solemn and agreeable sound of the organ. In this way I made my first acquaintance with Johann Sebastian Bach. He has been a true and faithful friend ever since.

I meet Johann Sebastian Bach.

Our Ancestors in General and My Own in Particular

THE NAZIS base their barbarous cruelty on the feeling of resentment caused by the iniquitous severity of the Treaty of Versailles. In this, as in most other instances, they are guilty of a deliberate lie. In the first place, the Treaty of Versailles, as peace treaties go, was not a bad one. It was infinitely more humane than the Treaty of Brest-Litovsk, which the victorious imperial armies had forced upon the defeated Russians. Of course, it was not a document of high ethical value, but what else could they have expected?

For four long years the Germans had murdered and burned and shot and hanged to their hearts' content. Now at last they had been defeated, and the world, licking its wounds, was in no mood to temper justice with mercy. But the spirit of revenge lasted a much shorter time than anyone had expected. The unpleasant old men who had been responsible for the Treaty disappeared, one after the other, from the stage, and Versailles became a dead letter. Meanwhile the Germans worked like beavers. After the war, the Reich had had only one passenger vessel fit for the Atlantic service. Soon it launched the *Bremen* and the *Europa* and a whole fleet of first-rate ships which began rapidly to take away the trade from its rival nations. The hotels, once more provided with such trifles as sheets and towels (immediately after the war there had been none), were so far superior to those in France and England (where the food, as of old, remained fit only for true Britons) that the traveling public hastened to visit the domains of the former enemy as if there never had been any war at all.

Meanwhile, the country was going through one of the most curious artistic, musical, and literary processes that has ever been observed in the history of civilized man. It is said (I have never had the opportunity to observe the truth of the statement) that a person on the point of drowning relives all the different periods of his life in the space of a few seconds. Germany, like a nation predestined to come to a violent end, went through just such a curious experience. One epoch followed the next with a rapidity and a thoroughness that no one has ever yet been able to explain. There was an era that so closely resembled the baroque that one might have thought oneself in the seventeenth century. Then there was a revival of the rococo and of the romantic period. Even the Middle Ages were not overlooked, and within the realm of the less pleasant aspects of life there was even a return to the perversions of the Greece of the fifth century B.C. And each one of those short intervals found expression not only in painting and etching, but in music and literature as well.

The undercurrent of Nazi muckerism was already making itself felt, but—if we are to be entirely fair about it—we must confess that this was the most glorious revival of the human mind the world had seen since the days of the Renaissance. This outbreak of artistic and intellectual enthusiasm did not by any means restrict itself to the purely historical aspects of the past. It also pushed itself vigorously forth into the future and gave us occasional glimpses of what lay just ahead of us, which made that more remote future quite attractive.

I cannot go into too much detail about this strange phenomenon—a whole nation suddenly busying itself in one last sublime effort to recapture in quick succession the spirit of its great past, just before it rushed forward towards a future I hate to contemplate. The periodicals that were printed during this period reflected that great intellectual revival. They became as interesting as our own were dull. Whereas the editors of our magazines seem to have but one purpose in life—never to touch (however remotely) upon a subject that a moron with a nickel in his pocket might not be able to understand—their German rivals of those twenty memorable years took the whole of creation as their province. They left the beaten path of the old and the tried, and boldly set out for the truth in whatever curious form or shape it might present itself.

I wish I had kept a few of those magazines, for they were full of fascinating topics about which we over here never seem to think or which we try to avoid, as they might lead to violent letters of protest on the part of our strongly organized minority groups. And what that means can only be appreciated by those editors who in some way have incurred the displeasure of the Church, the Jews, the Christian Scientists, the Irish, the Scotch (try and be funny about *Macbeth*), and all sorts of obscure groups of citizens, the existence of which they never even suspected until they flouted some cherished prejudice.

Somehow or other during the twenty years of that short-lived German Renaissance, the editors either seemed unaware of these minority groups or they just did not care, and printed whatever suited their fancy. In this, I think, they rendered a decided public service to the advancement of German culture, but of course our editors (who are always followers and never even pretend to be leaders) may have chosen the wiser part. For all those elements within the Reich which hated any kind of superior civilization (and Hitler very cleverly based his power upon those groups of intellectual malcontents) only bided their time, and, when they got into control, those magazines and those theatrical and artistic groups which had gone ultra-modern were brutally suppressed, their editors and managers either killed or sent to concentration camps, and such copies of printed matter as could be found, burned.

This is a fate that will hardly overtake our own *Saturday Evening Post* or *Cosmopolitan,* but future students of literature will pay a great deal of attention to the *Querschnitt* and the *Stachelschwein.* At best, they will look at the advertising pages of our popular monthlies and weeklies and will discard the rest as a waste of wood pulp, with its infantile stories and its serious articles which never go to the roots of any of the problems they discuss.

All this leads up to a short but very important article I found some ten years ago in one of those strange German monthlies. I saved it for quite a long time but lost it when the things I had stored in my native country were destroyed by the Germans, and I therefore have to reconstruct it from memory. The magazine discussed the problem of heredity and race, especially from the dynastic and aristocratic point of view, for in those days there were still a great many people who were deeply impressed by genealogies and purity of descent.

This is the way it reasoned in an effort to prove that there is no use in being so very superior about our own family tree, because all of us are really much more closely related to each other than we ever suspect.

We all of us have two parents, four grandparents, eight great-grandparents, sixteen great-great-grandparents, thirty-two great-great-great-grandparents, sixty-four great-great-great-great-grandparents, and so on and so forth until in the days of Christ's presence on earth, we must have had no fewer than 48,000,000,000,000,000 ancestors—that is forty-eight with fifteen zeros behind it. What that number must have been when Cheops built his pyramids in the twenty-ninth century B.C.! This, of course, is an absurdity, for the mortality among people until a hundred years ago was so great that even the

Chapter VI

number of inhabitants of such countries as England and France was ludicrously small, and Holland, during the seventeenth century, when it was in the heyday of its glory, had fewer than a million and a half people. Then what has become of those billions upon billions of ancestors of the two billion people who inhabit the world today, and whom I packed into my little box and pushed into the Grand Canyon in the foreword to my *Geography*? (This was also an idea I had found in a German publication.)

Nothing can have become of them, as they never existed except as first, second, third, or nineteenth cousins to the others. A few years ago in Sweden I saw a curious genealogical table of a really distinguished family. It was a round disk, the top of a glass-covered table. It began with Papa and Mamma in the center and then worked from the center outward, but already in the third layer one came upon the unavoidable cousins. Most of our 48,000,000,000,000,000,000 ancestors, therefore, were absorbed by their cousinquity—if I am allowed to express it that way. In plain and unvarnished language, we are all of us very closely related to each other; we are all of us cousins. This, of course, knocks the bottom out of that absurd myth of a pure race, which incidentally was not restricted to the half-wits of the Third Reich, but which, in a stranger or wilder form, had at times manifested itself in every other nation, our own included. It is funniest of all, however, in the case of Germany, which, starting out as a hopeless hodgepodge of Teutonic and Slavic races, was overrun during the Thirty Years' War by every kind of rabble from the rest of the European continent. And even among the more respectable invaders there was a great deal of non-Germanic blood.

The Swedes imported whole divisions of Finns, and the Finns were hardly Aryans. The imperial armies used all sorts of queer Balkan hirelings with very doubtful racial antecedents. And as these mercenaries had little direct interest in the religious issues for which they were supposed to be fighting, and were inspired only by a desire for loot and rape, the result from the point of view of maintaining a pure racial stock of German origin was extremely deplorable; and no sooner had some of the hideous damage caused by this senseless war been repaired (among other things it more than halved the population of Germany proper) than Napoleon appeared upon the scene. He preferred to let his foreign subject nations kill themselves rather than his beloved Frenchmen (the racial statistics upon his Russian campaign are most illuminating in this respect), and so the German plain was overrun by as motley a crew of Spaniards, Neapolitans, Tuscans, Umbrians, and Poles as was ever turned loose upon a defenseless population. Even Hans Christian Andersen, in his little town of Odense (and, God knows, in those days Spain was far removed from Denmark), was to be fascinated by those swarthy foreigners who used to pick him up in the street and kiss him and tell him about their own children in Andalusia. And if they kissed little boys, they probably also kissed a few not quite so young girls.

The myth, therefore, of a pure race to be found in any part of Europe belongs to the same wishful dreaming as is evinced in the first stanza of the national anthem of the Netherlands, where an appeal is made to all Dutchmen whose veins are free from foreign strains. There are no such veins, for the old Europe was as great a melting pot as the modern America.

It is interesting to note that this absurd myth about "racial purity" should have been revived by a half-breed German-Czech with possibly a Jewish strain. That, however, seems quite a common occurrence. The pure-race advocates of our own republic are only too often of the same doubtful antecedents as their great prophet of the Schicklgruber tribe.

I am happy to report that I grew up in an atmosphere which was most happily devoid of this kind of nonsense. Immediately after the foundation of the Dutch kingdom in the year 1813, there was a temporary outbreak of racial pride (the poor people had had so little to be proud of during the previous eighteen years of foreign subjugation), and there was a great to-do about the ancient Batavians, who, a century or so before Julius Caesar explored the wild west of the central European plain, were supposed to have settled among the marshes between the mouths of the Rhine and the Meuse. But when I was young, their name suggested nothing to us except a small amusement park between The Hague and Scheveningen, and the reference to our ancestral purity stressed in the national anthem meant even less, for that dull and ponderous poem had long since been parodied in doggerel of so extremely indecent a nature that I shall not even try to translate it. Children have a pretty fine nose for the phony, and the moment they feel that something is not entirely honest and genuine, they will turn the empty-sounding words of the uninspired poet into something so obscene that afterwards they themselves sometimes wonder how they could ever have been guilty of such sacrilege.

I don't know whether the Greeks indulged in that habit, but we have evidence that the Middle Ages did: exasperated scholars could recite reams of sacred literature without once using a proper word. But except for those rare official occasions when, neatly washed and brushed, we were supposed to listen to interminable orations by dull dominies and uninspired schoolteachers, we were at least spared the nightmare of being obliged to listen to those exhortations which even then were so common among our eastern neighbors, whose little boys and girls were forever being reminded of the virtues of Hermann, the leader of the Cherusci, and the noble Thusnelda, who undoubtedly looked like a Ukrainian peasant woman of a hundred years ago, when serfdom was still in flower.

When, therefore, I now pay my hasty respects to my ancestors (as I imagine them to have been), I do not reconstruct them from any data given me by my history teachers but rather from such information as I was able to collect later. They were a pretty sorry lot, and the miracle to me is that they ever survived the conditions under which they were obliged to live.

First of all, hundreds of thousands of years ago, they must have been among those low-browed savages whose skulls grinned at me from their showcases among the mummies of my pet museum in Rotterdam. They were dark-skinned, for we white-skinned folk are the queer-looking ones. We have no business to be as white as we are. We are freaks, the result, apparently, of having spent so many thousands of centuries in a climate that has affected our pigmentation until we look like caricatures of our former selves. And they were, of course, as messy as our own Indians at the time of their discovery by Signor Cristoforo Colombo of Genoa, Italy, of whom, for some mysterious reason, we always think as a Spaniard, although he was an Italian Jew, a circumstance which makes his fortunes and misfortunes much more understandable than if he had been a Catholic hidalgo.

They lived in a kind of nest or at best, like the present-day Australian aborigines, in a lean-to. Their offspring were brought up like the children of the Eskimos when they were still living in igloos. That is to say, from the moment they were born until the day of their death, they existed in the perpetual stench of accumulated offal and unwashed flesh. The death rate of these small creatures must have been terrific, but somehow they survived. Against the terrible animals which still populated the world, they had no other defense than their sticks and stones. But gradually they learned to sharpen those stones into knives and ax blades and spearheads, and the day the first knife was so neatly polished that it could cut the throat of a saber-toothed tiger, *Homo faber* took a much greater step forward along the road of progress than on the day James Watt set man free from his animal bondage by inventing an iron substitute for human muscles.

But between the crude and clumsy stone implements of the dawn man and the steellike daggers of the people who were still in existence when the Romans began to explore northern Europe, there elapsed a period far longer than the so-called historical era of the last four thousand years. In the meantime, as we now know with a reasonable amount of certainty, Europe had experienced a number of cold spells of such intensity and such long duration that the greater part of the continent lay covered underneath a heavy blanket of snow and ice. That was the period during which the human race went to school, for it was a question of invent or perish. And, as nobody likes to perish (the experience is so uncomfortably drastic and final), people began to use their brains and became great inventors.

They trained the wolf until it had become a most useful hunting companion. They found that the reindeer, ideally suited for conditions as they existed during the slow retreat of the glaciers, could be turned into a permanent source of supply for milk, meat, garments, and all sorts of bone implements from needles to skates. This creature, having an obstinate will of its own, never allowed itself to become quite so domesticated as the much less intelligent cow, but by following it during its peregrinations (as the Laplanders do to this day), its human fellow travelers were guaranteed against the everpresent danger of sudden starvation.

It must have been a strange world. I am glad I have seen enough of it to realize how little I should have liked it. When you look at a Lapp settlement way up in Sweden and think that once upon a time your glorious ancestors lived in that indescribable filth (though of course they had no gramophone with the latest rug-cutting melodies being endlessly repeated), you feel that, in spite of everything, we have come pretty far. Much farther indeed than we had any right to expect when we remember our very humble beginnings. For much was still to be accomplished after the first van Loons had decided to pull up stakes and, following in the footsteps of the slowly retreating glaciers, to occupy the unpopulated and barren wilderness of that part of the world lying north of the vast marshes that afterwards were to become the Mediterranean Sea.

The traces they left behind of their temporary stops along the banks of a number of rivers (usually those flowing between steep cliffs which offered a natural shelter) are so vague that we know nothing about their wanderings. Some, by following the Rhine, must have reached England. Gradually the lake to their north increased in size. In due course of time, it broke through the hills of the south, created what is today known as the English Channel, and also made a connection with the Arctic Sea, turning England into an island about which the rest of the world remained almost completely ignorant until, thousands of years later, a Roman explorer by the name of Julius Caesar visited these parts and found that he had to build himself a fleet if he wished to conquer the lands that lay westward of the open sea and about which the people in Rome knew less than we know today about the heart of Tibet or Brazil.

In the meantime, our own country had remained a land of trackless marshes, with a row of sand dunes protecting its swamps and bogs against the ravages of the North Sea. Here and there a small strip of land became fit for human habitation and attracted those types of immigrants who ever since the beginning of time have flocked to what today we call the frontier. There were a few hardy pioneers who hoped to find better living conditions for themselves and their families by pulling up stakes and moving into a part of the world where they could become independent huntsmen and traders. Judging by our own pioneers (whom since then we have scandalously idealized), some ten per cent or even less may have belonged among the more vigorous citizens who can make a success of such a venture. The rest belonged to two categories. The first comprised the weaker members of the tribe who could not make a go of it at home and who were forced to try their luck elsewhere. These either perished or attached themselves to a stronger neighbor, and soon were either out-and-out slaves or obliged to accept some kind of serfdom, if serfdom was already known to the people of prehistoric times. It probably was, though hardly under that name or as a recognized institution. For it seems to be a natural development of human society, and that is why, in a sense, we still have it with us today. Not officially, for in our day and age of triumphant democracy, we would violently deny that such a thing was possible. Those, however, who are familiar with the works of the excellent John Steinbeck will know better, and the others will never find out.

The second group was the criminal element which for safety's sake lost itself in this wilderness that it might continue its chosen profession under more favorable circumstances. Those, however, formed a negligible (if at times very uncomfortable) minority, for prehistoric jurisprudence must have closely resembled the law of the jungle, by which the herd promptly destroys whatever is dangerous to its own safety.

But of course I have no way of finding out whether my own ancestors belonged to those very early settlers or came at a later date. It is curious how the prehistoric type will maintain itself in spite of all crossbreeding. One day the Doctor, my beloved and learned uncle, and I were in a small village on the seacoast, when suddenly we stopped dead in our tracks. "My God!" we both said at the same moment. "A Neanderthaler!" And there he was, a full-blooded Neanderthaler: the receding brow, the long, apelike arms reaching down to below the knees, and the shambling gait that still is seen among the Irish in the more remote hamlets of Erin (undoubtedly because the weakest types among the prehistoric people of the mainland were forced away by the stronger ones and moved westward until they could go no farther, and the farthest westward, then as now, was western Ireland).

We made some discreet inquiries about our unexpected find and discovered that the man belonged to a family in which these characteristics were quite common. No, they were not exactly idiots, but they were esteemed borderline cases; at school they were always at the bottom of the class. They made a living as seashore scavengers, not having either the strength or the intelligence to qualify as regular fishermen. They were not in any way more viciously inclined than their neighbors, and, as they stuck very closely to their own kind and invariably married their cousins, nobody bothered about them, except that they were usually greeted with a cheerful, "Hiya, Ape!" which they did not in the least resent but on the contrary accepted as a sort of distinction, since they were the only people in the village who were known by that appellation.

I need not have had any fear, however, that we were descended from those walking prehistoric museum pieces, as my family (especially my mother's family) was well known for its good looks. My mother and my aunts had all of them been rather famous as beauties in their youth, and their brothers had a certain distinction which remained with them until the day of their death. Furthermore, all their racial characteristics pointed to a Saxon ancestry, although, of course, that ancestry must have been strongly tinctured with Frankish elements.

Those things, however, are of small historical importance. My grandfather hailed from Altenburg and therefore came from the old Germany of the days of Tacitus, which at the beginning of the Christian era stretched from the Rhine to the Elbe, the boundary between Teutons and Slavs.

The Frankish blood I deduce from my surname. In Dutch,

the predicate *van* does not have the same meaning as the *von* does in German. It is no indication of any kind of noble antecedent. It merely shows the village or the province from which a certain family came before it settled in a new community. In the Middle Ages everybody was known to his neighbors by his own name and that of his father. Jan the son of Jan became Jan Janszoon, and Klaas, the son of Klaas, became Klaas Klaaszoon. The same happened in the Scandinavian countries, and hence the astonishing numbers of Jensens and Pedersens in Minnesota. But during the sixteenth century, when the Dutch cities grew by leaps and bounds, this was no longer feasible, and families got to be classified according to the neighborhood from which they had come to the city to try their luck.

When I was about twelve years old (as I shall have to relate when I come to my chapter on our moving to The Hague), I suddenly developed a terrific interest in family trees and did my best to establish some direct relationship with the counts of Loon, one of whom, early in the thirteenth century, had married the reigning Countess of Holland and had laid claim to being recognized as the legitimate head of that then very important country. This gentleman had died while preparing for a pilgrimage to the Holy Land (for "preparing" read "getting a sufficient loan to pay for the trip"), and his wife had been banished to the island of Texel, for the nobles of Holland, who had greatly resented this foolish idea of being ruled by a woman and a foreign consort, had promptly thrown her out on her ear and had elected her uncle as her successor. As for the county of Loon, which fascinated me so greatly during the days I was an *Ivanhoe* fan, it had during the fourteenth century been absorbed by the neighboring bishops of Liége and had ceased to exist as an independent unit. There was not the slightest chance, therefore, of our being in any way connected with this feudal family, and I had to accept the fact (which then greatly humiliated me) that at an unknown date some honest baker or butcher had moved from the neighborhood of Loon to Rotterdam and had, on account of his "place of origin," become known as Jan or Piet from Loon, just as today my grandchildren in Vermont might be called "those kids from Connecticut" by their little Dorset schoolmates.

But as the county of Loon was in the Walloon part of Belgium, and as the Walloons are Franks rather than Saxons, I must have at least a modicum of Frankish blood in my rapidly aging veins.

As for the other strains, I have not the slightest idea, for how could we have kept any kind of record when even the Hapsburgs and the Hohenzollerns, who for centuries kept whole staffs of experts working at their family tree, never could push their descent much further back than at most the twelfth or eleventh century.

I once hired a poor scribe to go through the archives (in Holland, no official document has ever been known to be thrown away these last four hundred years, from dog licenses to royal wedding certificates) and dig up the van Loon begats. They had been a most respectable and extremely commonplace crowd of schoolteachers, ministers of the Gospel, and small proprietors, without a single person who had risen above the mediocre. But the more I have come to learn about conditions in the Low Countries during the first fifteen centuries of our era, the more I am surprised that they survived for a sufficiently long period to continue the van Loon tribe at all. The Romans probably did not affect them greatly. To them, this vast marshland was only important as the territory through which you had to pass as a gangway to Britain. Just as we, in the thirties and forties of the last century, constructed a chain of blockhouses along the trail to California so that the Indians could be kept within bounds by our cavalry, so did the Romans, following the course of the big rivers, erect their *castella* and leave a few hundred regulars and a couple of officers to look after the safety of the travelers, collect whatever taxes could be imposed upon the surrounding population, and bore themselves to death like those French officials whom before the war one met in Tahiti or Indo-China.

Our own military establishment in the Far West had a tendency to develop into trading stations where the natives gathered together to sell their produce and, if they were very lucky, to acquire a knife or a sword made of steel, for most of them still lived in the stone age or at best had progressed as far as iron.

I have sometimes tried to imagine what one of my ancestors (for my mother's people may well have been there at that time) of this Roman period might have looked like. Probably he was not unlike the sort of Injuns one still found at an Indian trading post in Oklahoma thirty years ago: not too bright, not too clean, not too sober (if he could help it), and a lazy bum who let his wife do all the work unless it were a question of fighting or hunting, in which case he would become almost animated. The noble-savage ideal, as it referred to the ancient Germanic tribes of northern Europe, came much into vogue some sixty years ago and was developed in a number of historical novels that now have been most fortunately forgotten. I don't want to seem unduly hard on them, but I have, I think, one great advantage over the distinguished authors of that period, when Roman wickedness was forever being compared to virtue as practiced by the fair-haired, blue-eyed heroes of the forests dedicated to Wotan. I have acquired some firsthand knowledge of these glorious savages and have found them pretty terrible. I do not refer to a race or color different from our own. One of the greatest gentlemen it was ever my privilege to meet was a full-blooded Zulu in the heart of Natal, but he had been exposed to the white man's ways in that one respect which sometimes seems the only excuse for our colonizing activities—our insistence upon a certain amount of neatness in our personal behavior.

I am not, however, going to indulge in that strange philosophy (not uncommon among us) which identifies civilization with bathtubs. The garbage can, to my way of thinking, is a much greater step forward along the road of progress than the bathtub, and what horrifies me most of all in the lives of primitive people is the physical messiness of their daily existence, which seems to exercise a very direct influence on their way of thinking. I therefore can only bless the day when the Romans, with several thousand years of Mediterranean civilization behind them, reached our ancestral marshes.

I remember how, not so many years ago, in a small island of the Netherlands East Indies, I noticed a woman in the local hospital—a woman whose entire head was swathed in bandages. I asked the doctor if she had been in an accident. "No," he answered, "her husband returned from a hunting trip, and she refused him what are politely called his 'conjugal rights.' So he tried to cut off her nose and ears, for that was according to local usage. She lived in a village some ten hours away from here, but we somehow got her to this hospital. I think we shall save her, and we have done a pretty good plastic job."

"And the husband?"

"We got him too."

"And what will you do to him?"

"What can we do? We shall put him on the chain gang for a year or so, and he will be quite contented, for he will have his board and lodging for nothing. Then he will go free."

"And the woman?"

"She will go back to him. What else is there for her in a community like this?"

I knew there was nothing else for that woman in such a community, and I also realize my own ancestors were probably

little better before the coming of the Roman law. It undoubtedly interfered with the freedom of action of the native, but I
have never heard a reasonable explanation of what there was
wrong with this arrangement. Just now there seems to be another movement to compare the white man's ways with those
of his duskier brethren, and invariably it is the white man who
comes off second best. I am thoroughly familiar with the less
pleasing and the more bestial qualities of those creatures (the
whaler and the trader) who were the precursors of the white
man's invasion of the Atlantic, the Pacific, and the Arctic
regions. But those who accuse him of having invaded a terrestrial paradise and ruthlessly destroyed the blissful existence
of millions of innocent little boys and maidens had better study
the subject a little more carefully. Even the Pacific, where
nature provided a background of almost unearthly loveliness
and where man was more or less free from the fear of want
(you can never really get very hungry if you live next to a
coconut tree), was so full of irrepressible anthropophagous
appetites and all sorts of sadistic cruelties, practiced upon both
friends and enemies, that it was on the way to depopulating
itself long before Captain James Cook appeared upon the
scene and himself was slain for his troubles.

I am therefore grateful to Julius Caesar and his legionaries
for having discovered my ancestors and for having taught them
a few things they probably would not have learned by themselves: how to build dikes and how to construct drainage canals,
so that they might at last live in comparative safety from the
violence of the ever-destructive waters of the ocean and begin
to cultivate little patches of grain and keep a few cows and
chickens. And I am sorry that bad management at home forced
the Romans from their British colony, in which they had lived
for more years than the white man has been in America.

For with the disappearance of the Roman traffic cop and the
Roman magistrate and the Roman engineer, it was as if they

had never been at all. Great-grandpa speedily reverted to his old and reprehensible ways. He had no longer the well-arranged Roman villa to excite his envy and make him wish for a home like that himself someday. He was content to live in a single room without window or chimney and thought nothing of sharing it with his pigs, his children, and his wife. He neglected his dikes and let the big rivers have their way until the central part of those territories he considered his own particular domain were turned into a vast inland sea—that so-called Zuyder Zee which, after an independent and more or less turbulent existence of some fifteen centuries, is at last being reminded that it was not so much an act of nature as the result of human carelessness and that therefore it had better let itself be dried up and return to its original destiny as a provider of food for man and beast.

As for the roads which for well-nigh half a thousand years had seen a steady procession of merchants and merchandise, they were left to be the prey of the highwayman until the Punic traders from the south no longer ventured forth into those barbarous regions and the women lost their colorful cotton garments and their trinkets and those popular cosmetics the (perhaps crude) use of which they had learned from the wives of the officers of the Roman legions.

In short, there was an immediate and speedy return to the primitive ways of their barbaric ancestors, and with the tribal medicine men once more in charge of the sick, the Greek physicians who had accompanied the armies of the invaders no longer felt it safe to practice their trade and returned whence they had come.

It is astonishing how little time it takes to revert to barbarism. This was shown after the end of the Thirty Years' War in 1648 (Harvard College had already existed a dozen years), when the people of some of the most plundered sections of Germany once more began to practice anthropophagy, which is a beautiful Greek word for the eating of human flesh. And soon all that part of Europe might have sunk back into the savagery that was observed and regretted by Tacitus, when he visited those regions during the first century of our era, if it had not been for the advent of a number of courageous men who were so completely filled with the message of hope and love they meant to carry unto the ends of the earth that they did not mind the perils and discomforts connected with their missions. They boldly penetrated into every nook and corner of this unknown territory to tell the gaping natives about the mysterious new God who had come to save them. He Himself had met death at the hands of that same emperor whose legions their ancestors had so successfully destroyed in the ever-famous battle of the Teutoburger Wald. * This encounter, it is true, had been one of those freak battles like the so-called massacre of General Custer, and had not prevented the Romans from establishing themselves along the right bank of the Rhine. But it was one of the few things the Teutonic tribes of the north still remembered—for on that day the German had proved himself superior to the Roman.

As for the new God's highly curious doctrine that you must love everybody (including, of all people! your enemies and those who had done you wrong), it took these northern savages a long time to accept the happy tidings without a fierce feeling of resentment which usually showed itself by falling upon the intruders who wanted to make mollycoddles of their sons and by sending them to that paradise of which they had spoken so eloquently while setting fire to shrines their own fathers had in bygone days erected to Wotan and Freya.

------

* Here, in A.D. 9, the Roman legions under Varus were utterly defeated by the German tribes under Hermann (Arminius).—Ed.

Among the Early Christians

FOR A great many years I have played with the idea of writing a history book that should deal with my ancestors from the first century until the present—as I imagined them, of course, for facts I had none. The period that puzzled me most of all was that period, from the beginning of the seventh to the end of the eighth centuries, during which our own part of the world was converted to Christianity. At school, I had been taught that it had all been very nice and easy. Of course, here and there a few wild Frisians had behaved in a most deplorable manner by occasionally hacking a couple of pious missionaries to death, just as (hundreds of years later) the aborigines of New Guinea would now and then descend upon a Christian settlement and go home happily displaying their collection of fresh white skulls. But the affair would soon be settled by the arrival of a gunboat, and justice would be done by slaughtering a couple of hundred natives. That was, as we were told, one of the advantages of a strongly centralized government, and, not having the slightest idea what "colonial administration" meant (except when one of our own relatives was among the victims), we had right heartily agreed and had duly learned our lessons by heart. "A.D. 630: Dagobert builds a chapel in Utrecht. A.D. 679: the Frisian king Radbad destroys the chapel which Dagobert had founded in Utrecht. A.D. 754: Boniface, the missionary to the Frisians, is murdered while preaching the Gospel."

Chapter VII

But dates meant about the same thing to us then as vitamin pills mean to my grandchildren. We swallowed them and forgot about them as soon as convenient, which meant immediately after the last examination just before the long vacation. Then in the fall, when we returned to our dull classroom, we started out once more. A.D. 630: Dagobert founds a chapel in Utrecht. A.D. 679: the Frisian king Radbad destroys the chapel which Dagobert had founded in Utrecht, etc., etc. The same old story every year, but a little more elaborate as we grew older and were supposed to have a better understanding of such things. In the end, we were also told of the growth of monasticism and how the good monks everywhere repaired the dikes, taught the people how to raise more and better vegetables, and even persuaded them to refrain from murdering one another during Lent and between Monday morning and Wednesday evening of every week, and how these same monks set an example to their unruly neighbors by treating their slaves and serfs much more decently than did other owners of these human cattle.

But how this came about, this sudden change from an abandoned paganism to an enlightened Christianity, that was a detail which was never explained to us—as I understand now, because the process was so hopelessly complicated and so many-sided that the average public-school teacher himself had not the slightest idea how it came about and found it much easier to let us recite: "A.D. 630: Dagobert builds a chapel in Utrecht. A.D. 679: the Frisian king Radbad destroys the chapel which Dagobert had founded in Utrecht."

Sometimes, to enliven the story, they would tell the yarn about this same King Radbad. It seems that this wicked heathenish Frisian chieftain had finally met his just reward and had fallen into the hands of the forces of law and order. It remained unexplained where those forces of law and order had suddenly come from, but there they were and, being full of law and order, had placed before the King the choice of either letting himself be baptized or losing his head. His Majesty, being a sensible person, had expressed a preference for baptism. But when he already had one foot in the baptismal font (it was never explained to us that this must have been a river or a pool), he drew back and asked whether, in case he received baptism, he would go to heaven. He was assured that he would.

"And if I refuse to accept baptism?"

In that case, he was informed, he would go to hell.

"Well," he was supposed to have answered, "you might just as well cut my head off and let me go to hell. For there, at least, I will spend eternity with my own friends; whereas, if I go to heaven, I won't know a soul."

The purpose of this story, I am sure, was to make us see what an obstinate and wicked old man this King Radbad had been, but we children rather liked him for his decision to lose his head and stick to his friends. Of course, we never said so, for it would have meant a bad mark, and we would have been deprived of our liberty and compelled to stay at home and learn our lessons a little better.

Today I am no longer obliged to worry about either A's or E's (except such as my readers give me), but I am just about as far removed from understanding the quick and comparatively easy conversion of these hundreds of thousands of people from the old to the new faith as I was at the age of eight. I have, however, accumulated a few guesses which I shall now offer.

I am sure that it was not a question of "seeing new great light," as I was taught afterwards in my catechism. And considerations of an ethical and spiritual nature had even less to do with it. All these endless Saxons and Frisians and Sicambri, or whatever their names may have been, were no more interested in the spiritual values of life than the head-hunters of central Borneo are today. They had their own "rules of conduct" that they had inherited from their fathers, as those in turn had inherited them from theirs and so on back through the ages and into the dim past of their dark and gory Valhalla. As a result, their daily conduct remained about the same as it had been before their conversion. They continued to fight among themselves, to behave like gangsters towards the unfortunate traders who set foot on their soil, to let their wives do most of the work around their clearings, and to drink and gamble to excess. Occasionally, they would even plunder a cloister. But now that I have a much better perspective upon this most interesting episode in the white man's history, I am beginning to understand what an infinite amount of good was done by the Christianization of these barbarians.

The Christian faith, when it finally reached this part of the European frontier, was already seven hundred years old, which is pretty old as religions go. I now have a fairly clear idea of why it had triumphed over all its rivals, for let us remember that the Rome of early imperial days was as full of competing mysteries as the New York of today. The old gods were still officially alive, but most people no longer took them very seriously. They had become personages in fairy stories connected with the earliest days of the race. A "modern" Roman no longer expected to meet Pan while walking through the fields, and Jupiter was a name by which you swore but not a deity whom you worshiped. However, since these gods and goddesses were entirely interwoven with the official life of the state, it was considered good policy to continue them in office. And so the Romans went through their ceremonies, just as today our liberals (who are no longer Christians in the more serious sense of the word) will let a minister marry them and baptize their children and bury them because it is the thing to do, and otherwise the neighbors might start talking or asking questions.

Meanwhile the Romans, and especially the Roman women, found a way out for their emotional life, going for all the fads that had gradually found their way to the world's metropolis. Greek and Syrian and Egyptian and Chaldean and Persian spook doctors and soothsayers were reaping a golden harvest with their foreign hocus-pocus. They were as clever as our own astrologers, numerologists, and fortunetellers and had a great and, on the whole, most nefarious influence upon society at large. For many of the boys were past masters at all the subtler perversions of the Orient, and conditions in Rome gradually began to resemble the Berlin of republican days, where the morals of a great part of the people had been so completely ruined that, from that angle at least, a strong regime had become an absolute necessity.

Meanwhile, the Empire, while it had undoubtedly established a state of law and order which had "made the trains run on time" (as we used to say about Mussolini and his Fascists in the twenties and early thirties), had done remarkably little for the comfort and happiness of the average citizen. Like the Russia of czarist days, it was a mixture of unwarranted luxury for the few and bottomless misery for the many. The endless wars of conquest had filled the nation with such an overabundance of military prisoners that almost seventy per cent of the population consisted of slaves. The fate of these creatures was not a happy one, for they could be bought a dozen for a dollar, so to speak, and were treated as our little boys and girls used to treat their bicycles before the outbreak of the present war, when Papa and Mamma took them away and used them to go to the village.

Inside the regular community the slaves therefore formed a community which had to live without that which alone makes life bearable—hope. They were considered of so little importance that they were not even allowed to take part in the religious ceremonies of the state. Like the pariahs of our own time, they were in this world but not of it. And then one day they heard rumors—vague whisperings at first—about a new

Messiah who had come to this earth to tell all people that they were children of the same father—that there was a heaven where all of them would have an equal chance of salvation— that the poor had a better chance to find favor in the eyes of the Almighty than the rich—in short, that after death they would enter upon a new life in which none of the values of the old one were any longer valid because it was the realm of the poor, the humble, and the meek.

The Roman Empire of the first century of our era was not exactly a place in which the poor, the humble, and the meek enjoyed much of a chance. The disinherited masses sat up and took notice, and as soon as they had an opportunity they sneaked off to some clandestine meeting of the followers of the new Messiah to listen to the stories of those who had either known him or had known someone who had heard him preach among the barren hills of the distant land of Palestine. And not only were they received like brethren and sisters, but they were able to share the simple communal meals of their new friends, who despised all material possessions, who claimed that a rich man had much less chance at salvation than a camel has to pass through the eye of a needle, and who were eager to share their wealth with all their neighbors.

But more than the communistic aspects of the new faith, it must have been the element of hope that made the masses flock in ever-increasing quantities to the foot of that cross on which their Leader had been nailed like a runaway slave, for cruci- fixion was the punishment the Romans meted out to runaway slaves and to those who dared to mutiny against the imperial authority.

The whole atmosphere, therefore, in which Jesus had lived and died was familiar to the slave population of the empire. It was their own atmosphere and background. A single ill- guarded remark to a cruel master or his supercilious mistress could carry them to the cross. Let them lift a hand against a brutal overseer who had thrashed one of their children (if they were allowed to have their children with them) and the cross awaited them. And here was a simple carpenter from an obscure village who while on earth had always associated with fishermen and tavern keepers and other humble folk, both men and women, who had somehow incurred the displeasure of the authorities by his very love for the poor, and who had been killed by them, as they would destroy anyone rash enough to question the established order of things.

Yes, this was not the case of some remote god like that Mithras who was now so popular among the Roman soldiers that he had almost completely replaced old Jupiter. This was no Cybele, with her silver body and her head of black stone, driving her lion-drawn chariot on the way to her lover. This was no Carthaginian deity who headed the beastlike gods of that now forgotten city—dreadful creatures with bristly bellies like those of swine. Nor did He in any way resemble that Dionysus who had recently become so popular because his priests sold powerful aphrodisiacs and his priestesses operated regular bordellos. And finally (for times had changed) He did not demand that He be worshiped by the spilling of real blood and flesh—a practice that seemed to appeal most of all to the fashionable ladies of the Via Claudia and of the hills of Tusculum. A few drops of wine and a small morsel of bread, reverently swallowed by those who wished to honor His memory—that was all that could remind students of the days when a Baal-berith or a Baal-zebub was still allowed to have his statues in every city and village of Syria and Palestine and when the altars of these honorable demons were forever dripping with the blood of recently massacred men and women.

In the beginning a great many people, not knowing much about the Jews, who by now had settled down in every city of the Mediterranean, thought of the Christians as members of some kind of refined Jewish sect which had dropped a few of the old strict laws about eating and drinking and going to bed and getting up and shaving your wife's head after you had married her and cooping the women up in a separate part of your temples and not working when everybody else was working and working when nobody else worked and not allowing a single stranger to spend a night within the walls of your holy town and not having any converse (if you could possibly avoid it) with a fellow citizen who had not submitted to the rite of circumcision. If in their ignorance about this Jewish exclusiveness such seekers after the new truth found their way to the synagogue the Hebrew immigrants had built in their town, they were soon made to understand that they had come to the wrong place. They were spat at the moment they mentioned the name of that Jewish prophet about whom they wanted to learn more details. Angry voices denounced this traitor to his own race, and they were threatened with stones and sticks unless they left the premises, for the Jews bitterly hated this false Messiah who had so far forgotten the law of his fathers as to associate with non-Jews on a footing of absolute equality, who would heal the sick daughter of a Gentile woman as readily as if she had been a Jewess, who would as willingly pass the time of day and break bread with a foreigner as with a member of his own tribe, who would address himself just as happily to the common people as to the Scribes, and who had not even hesitated to state (in public, too) that there were certain laws of humanity which far surpassed the taboos and restrictions laid down a thousand years before by the great Moses.

Having thus learned by experience that Judaism and Christianity were two very different things, the seekers after the new mystery would then eventually find their way to the house of a baker or an oil dealer, where in a dark little room they could listen to some itinerant preacher who explained the mystery of the plain man who had come to bring hope and salvation to those who had been cast out by life—to the slaves, the disinherited, the simple of mind, the plain, everyday folk of the slums and the slave quarters.

All this I have since then learned, and today I see it very clearly, just as I can see why twelve centuries later a man like Francesco Bernardone could make so many people give up everything that they might follow him and just as I know that the same thing would happen today if another Joshua of Nazareth or Francis of Assisi should come along and, having the courage of his convictions, should tell the multitudes that they were looking for salvation in the wrong direction and that it is not what he has that will make a man happy, but that his riches consist in the things he can do without. But the Jesus who was evolved out of those early days of a simple faith and unquestioning acceptance, out of the kind and cheerful teacher who had presided over the common gatherings of his disciples, who had lived their own simple life, who had wandered through the fields of Judea with them, and who, after the cool of the evening had set in, had entertained them with his wise parables and his little stories about true happiness and true righteousness—that new Jesus of the fourth and fifth centuries of our era, a full-fledged God, even more complicated than the deities of the ancient Babylonians (who were the first to have invented the idea of the Trinity), as remote and unapproachable as the old Jehovah of the Jews, a miracle worker *in absentia* and the object of a very material and highly physical form of worship—Him I never understood and with Him I never had any desire to hold converse. It took me a great many years of rather hard work to find out how He had come into being. That was only natural, for I had tried to reach Him via Rome when I should have chosen the road that led through Constantinople.

But who had ever dreamed of teaching us any Byzantine history? That curious and highly interesting Eastern Empire might just as well never have existed as far as we Dutch children were concerned. About the only date connected with it in our minds was the year 1453, when it fell into the hands of the Turks, and Europe became blessed with its everlasting and unsolvable Balkan problem. We were then told that the last of the Byzantine emperors had died fighting bravely on the steps of Aya Sofia and were given the wholly erroneous information that it had meant "the introduction of Greek scholars and Greek writers into Europe." This fable still persists. I find it in a little history book of my grandchildren, and nothing was ever farther from the truth, for the Byzantine professors, having long since read the handwriting on the walls of their fast-crumbling city, had already made it a habit to become guest stars at various European universities, where their knowledge of the Greek tongue had been a most welcome addition to the regular curriculum. And neither had the fall of the Byzantine capital been an event of such importance as we were made to believe. The Turks were already in Europe when Constantine IX died, and his capital had been reduced to a small Christian island in the midst of a sea of infidels. But the existence of that curious theocracy (in which the emperor had been the head of both the church and the state, as he was afterwards in Russia) had been a fact that most decisively influenced the history of Europe, and about that we had never learned a thing.

Today it matters very little politically whether the Eastern half of the Roman Empire continued for ten or for a thousand years. But the way in which it influenced our own religious conceptions, especially the figure of the Christ, is something that is still very much with us and will continue to be for a great many centuries to come. And as I see it, it was by no means a happy influence, for Christianity became the official religion of the Eastern half of the Roman Empire (the only part that survived) at a moment when the old Greek world (and Byzantium, we should always remember, was a Greek state, not a Latin one) had long since outlived its own usefulness and had sunk into a state of such complete intellectual, spiritual, and moral decay that it was like a stagnant pool which could still reflect ancient glory but which was so full of all sorts of unhealthy creatures that it could only spread death among those who came in contact with it.

I know that there is a school of historians who deny this and who claim that Byzantium, for the first five centuries of its existence at least, was a vigorous center of civilization—the recognized metropolis of the Mediterranean world. But anyone who has ever experimented with a melting pot (or a good goulash for that matter) knows that the final product does not depend so much upon your skill (the stuff will melt anyway) as upon the ingredients that have been thrown into it. And Byzantium (or Constantinople, or Istanbul, if you want to be very modern), which was the outstanding melting pot of the ages, even more so than Venice afterwards, had not been fortunate in the material that history had dropped into this racial caldron, which had already been stewing for some centuries when Romulus and Remus finally decided to found a little city of their own on the Tiber.

Ports of entry are rarely hotbeds of virtue, for there are always quite a number of people who find it necessary to leave one country for another (some little item like murder, fraud, rape, larceny, or an inability to pay one's debts), and they have an unfortunate habit of clinging closely where they first set foot on the new soil. In the end, such harbors have become veritable breeding places of every kind of criminality and vice. If, in addition to being a port of entry, such a city is the center of an empire and happens to be situated on the main highroad between two continents, then the result is likely to surpass our greatest expectations. And when, in addition to all this, it has developed into a center for all the cults, faiths, beliefs, and frauds of a thousand different peoples from the Himalayas to the Atlas Mountains and from the banks of the Tagus to those of the Volga, then you have got something that will make the witches' kettle of *Macbeth* look like a cup of weak tea being boiled over a sterno burner in a Greenwich Village hall bedroom.

The names of all the races that contributed to this evil-smelling *pot-au-feu* are not equally meaningful to our modern ears. There were Slavs and Greeks and Anatolians and Thracians and Macedonians and Venetians and Genoese and Circassians and Norsemen. After the battle of Hastings, there was a sudden influx of English refugees, most of whom became officers of the imperial guard and married Byzantine ladies of high estate. There were people from the islands of the Aegean Sea and from the Nile delta, and there were blackamoors from every part of Nubia, as Africa was then known. There were Persians and Indians of every kind and description, and even the slant-eyed, inscrutable men from distant Cathay were present to sell the court its precious silk robes. There were Babylonians and Syrians. Jews had put in an early appearance, and so had refugees from Carthage and Syracuse and every other city that had been captured and destroyed during the last thousand years.

And this human conglomeration was ruled over by emperors, most of whom had not a drop of either Latin or Greek blood in their veins, but who were military gangsters from the Slavic or Mauretanian hinterland and who were apt to marry women who seemed to have come straight out of a play by Victorien Sardou. To make matters even more complicated from our Western point of view, this curious state was ruled by eunuchs. Not only were the guards of the women's quarters recruited from among the mutilated children of the near-by mountaineers, but such children brought a much higher price in the Constantinople market place than normal ones and were therefore as systematically cultivated as they were afterwards in Italy by ambitious and greedy peasants who in this way hoped to see their sons become famous sopranos in the papal choir (the practice was finally abolished by Leo XIII) or at the London opera house, where my own grandfather heard the last one sing.

In Byzantium, however, eunuchs were preferred for the civil service and (incredible though it may seem) not infrequently led the emperor's armies or navies. They also were the private teachers of the sons and daughters of the rich and noble and sometimes married them, a practice as old as the days of the pyramids; for Captain Potiphar, famous to all of us through the story of Joseph, was a eunuch, and we should therefore not blame the lady so severely as we usually do. They were so greatly preferred as officers of the state that many influential families took the precaution of having their male children castrated that they might have a better chance of promotion. Narses, who at the age of seventy-five annihilated the Gothic hordes which had invaded northern Italy, was a eunuch and the first of a whole series of generals and admirals of the same variety. Indeed, there was only one single office to which no *castrato* dared aspire. He could never become emperor. On several occasions, the widows of a number of emperors tried to have their pet eunuchs elevated to the throne. But at this the church authorities and the senate drew the line. The emperor's son, at least, had to be an "entire man."

All this sounds messy and nauseating, and why bring it up, as it has little or no connection with the early history of a small Dutch boy? Outwardly it has none, but there is an inner connection, for it was in this unsavory atmosphere that the conception of Christ as a god and not as the greatest moral teacher of all times developed and became so definitely set that it is still one of the main obstacles to His Church's becoming truly Christian.

CHAPTER VIII

A Long Digression, Chiefly on Matters Monastic

A GREAT deal of water had flowed through the Bosporus, and tens of thousands of ships had dropped anchor in the Golden Horn, since the ancient Greek philosophers at the foot of their "warbling rock"—the home of the learned and illustrious goddess Athena—had stouteartedly taken the universe in hand and had examined all matters pertaining to the human race in order to discover the secret source that made the universe operate the way it did. A barbarian chieftain had destroyed the old and independent communities where the soul of man had been as free as his body, unless, of course, he was a slave, but then he did not count any more than did the donkeys in the stables.

Next, Greece had become a Roman province and, bereft of its former trade, had degenerated into that which Italy was in the days of my own youth—a sight-seer's paradise, the happy hunting ground of those who could not make both ends meet at home ("Such wonderful servants, my dear, and they work for nothing!"), a glorified picture postcard, and a source of riches for the publishers of guidebooks.

But it happened at the same time that the Romans, now having conquered most of the world and sitting pretty, so to speak, on top of their accumulated wealth, began to feel the need of something which today we would call "culture," and, being a people given to doing things rather than to thinking thoughts, they were sadly aware of their own shortcomings in the realm of the mind.

Now they discovered Greece as one vast academy of learning. The Platos and the Aristotles and all the other great philosophers and compilers of wisdom were dead and gone, but the academies in which they had taught survived and were still used as mental training schools by professional pedagogues who bore about the same resemblance to the philosophers of the classical era as the painters and architects of modern Italy do to their predecessors of the age of the Renaissance.

The Roman, a man of very limited powers of imagination, did not realize this, and for almost half a thousand years he sent his sons to Athens that there, in the atmosphere of true erudition, they might achieve the education they could not obtain at home.

The result was equally disastrous for both the teachers and their pupils, but it was perhaps the professors who suffered most, for they knew only too well who buttered their bread for them, and they soon gave their young charges what the young charges themselves wanted rather than what they needed. And soon the crystal-clear form of reasoning of the Greeks of the Periclean age was thoroughly degraded by the compromises of the inferior minds who then conducted Greece's most popular schools.

In the meantime, the cities that Alexander the Great had founded in other parts of his empire had developed into very prosperous commercial centers, and, since learning, like art, will always follow the full dinner pail, hungry *Privatdozenten* and unsuccessful coaches of mathematics and languages and philosophy hastened to the southern shores of the Mediterranean, there to set up shop and teach the sons of rich Egyptian merchants as their betters at home taught those who came to them from Rome.

Chapter VIII

The result was a rapid deterioration of the art of learning, and, just as Rome had gradually become filled with all sorts of new and outlandish cults, religions, and superstitions, so the whole educational fabric of the old world became more and more corrupted. Straight and hard thinking disappeared from the face of the earth, and its place was taken by the crookedest and most complicated system of mental hairsplitting the world had ever seen.

A thousand angels were not yet dancing on the point of a needle, but they would soon be doing so, for now the old Byzantium had become Nova Roma or Constantinople (as the Emperor encouraged his subjects to call it) and, as the seat of what remained of the old imperial government, it had become the one spot where a bright and energetic and not overscrupulous young man might hope to make a very comfortable living as a private tutor or secretary to some powerful politician in need of a polyglot aide to attend to his correspondence with every part of His Majesty's highly polyglot domains.

All of this happened because, in the year 306, one Flavius Valerius Constantinus, a former governor of Britain, had been acclaimed Caesar and, realizing that the once despised Christians had now become the most dependable and the best-organized minority in his turbulent empire, had made common cause with them and at length had made Christianity the official religion of the state. This had been purely a matter of practical necessity, for the emperor himself did not accept baptism until he was on his deathbed, when a great many people feel suddenly moved to take out such insurance against eternal perdition. Especially was this so of the illegitimate son of a Roman emperor and a Bithynian woman, for he had the death of many of his relatives, including his wife, on his conscience. Nor had he ever given any evidence of understanding the real meaning of any of Christ's words. For no sooner had he assumed the royal purple than he tried to re-establish that emperor worship which was one of the main things to which the Christians in old Rome had objected and the cause of much of the persecution they had suffered.

But the leaders of the Christian faith had not been unaware of the advantages they might derive from having their creed so closely interwoven with the political fabric of the state, and when Constantine decided to break entirely away from ancient Rome (the democratic traditions of which he loathed and despised) and build a new center of government on the site of the old city of Byzantium (which had commanded the road from Asia to Europe for more than a thousand years), they made common cause with their former enemy, and from that moment on Christ ceased to be the companion of the meek and the humble and those in distress—the healer of lacerated bodies and souls—and became an active partner in one of the most autocratic, tyrannical forms of government that history records.

His exact status and powers were definitely established by a series of synods, and even the number of hairs which could be shown on His hand in an icon was duly prescribed by an act of council. This process of petrifaction had become an accomplished fact some three centuries before His creed was at last carried to those districts then inhabited by my ancestors. That is to say, they did not meet the itinerant preacher who had hoped to cure man's ills by His example of love, understanding, and compassion, but the Christ of the Council of Nicaea—a stern ruler surrounded by imperial pomp and cut off from all direct contact with those who wished to adore Him by a priesthood that acted as bodyguard and executor of His commands.

In all fairness it must be granted that such a Christ was infinitely more understandable and acceptable to the heathen of twelve centuries ago than the other one who had first inspired the lovalty and devotion of so many million men and women when in Him they had found the leader who could draw them away from the tribulations and worries of their miserable everyday lives and who could inspire them to practice righteousness for righteousness' sake. They were to meet the Christ of the Gospels some eight hundred years later. They were then to make the greatest of personal and public sacrifices to perpetuate what they believed to be the true meaning of the tidings He had brought to this world. But in the days when the first Christian missionaries made their appearance, they were still too hopelessly lacking in any of the finer perspectives of life's inherent possibilities to have any understanding of the ethical aspects so prominent in the teachings of the Nazarene teacher. And when we hear of the wholesale and forcible conversion of the tribes then inhabiting northern Europe, we can take that statement in the most literal sense of the word.

The old gods no longer counted for much among these people. Any person in an elevated position has to learn the art of keeping the rest of the world at a distance. Hence etiquette, that elaborate ceremonial by which the anointed person is kept in a state of dignified aloofness from the multitude. And the ancient Teutons had come to know the intimate gossip concerning their deities just a shade too well to be any longer very much impressed by them. They were not actually hostile to them but they had become slipshod in their attitude. And they also felt that their own gods had treated them rather shabbily while they were trying to defend their lands against the foreigners from the south. Jupiter had invariably proved himself more powerful than Wotan, and the Mithras of the Roman legionaries was a better general than Thor. And so why any longer put your faith in those who were apparently unwilling or unable to help you, when there were other gods just as good or better? And the new deity offered concrete advantage over all the others. His priests were practical fellows, well trained in a great many things that contributed to your own well-being and comfort.

We should remember that one of the reasons the benighted heathen of every part of the world have always fallen so easily for the white man's ways lies in just that fact—the white man leads an infinitely less difficult existence than the black man or the yellow man. He has learned how to tame the forces of nature—he is no longer a beast of burden. He can sit in the shade of his porch and push buttons that make water turn into wine. He can kill his enemies at a distance of miles, and even the lightning of heaven will do his bidding and slip quietly into the earth without setting his house on fire. He can wireless a message that otherwise would take days of heavy trudging to deliver. The white intruder, therefore, is to them a man of miracles, and they envy him and want to find out how he does his tricks.

These miracle-makers came to the heathen of northern Europe in the guise of monks, and it is difficult for us, who may never have met a single monk in all our days, to imagine what a part they played in the spread of the Christian faith during the first twelve hundred years of our era. For after the end of the thirteenth century their job had been done, and they survived as a social nuisance rather than a social benefit. But during the first six centuries the Church would never have got anywhere at all without those shock troops who were at the same time the engineers and the medical corps and the administrative department.

There was nothing new in the idea of taking yourself out of the turmoil of daily life and finding a happier existence in keeping to your own devices, without being bothered by homes or spouses or children, or by the sheriff and the bailiff asking you to pay bills for articles you never should have bought. The Romans had had their vestal virgins, young women who preferred to remain virgins and be protected from the evil forces of this world by dedicating themselves to the service of the goddess Vesta, a lady of Greek import, and patroness of the domestic hearth. The Persians had nuns—women who made the sacred feathered garments that were used in the worship of the sun. Buddhism had its monks, and they were found all over China. The Jews had, among their many sects, one known as the Essenes, who in the second century B.C. practiced all those virtues of poverty, common ownership of all property, celibacy, and Sabbath-keeping which we now associate with the ideals of the monastic life. Indeed, they were so far removed from life as it was lived by their neighbors that both Jesus and John the Baptist were suspected of being Essenes in disguise.

Monasticism (or the custom of "living alone") therefore greatly outdated Christianity and was a phenomenon which in all parts of the world had been born of an identical desire to escape from the uncongenial realities of a far from perfect world. Enthusiasm for this sort of life will therefore at all times largely depend upon general conditions. In present-day America, where the average boy still has a good many chances (if not quite so many as before) to go out and hustle for himself and get a job and marry the girl who wants him and become a useful citizen of the community in which he settles down and see his own kids do likewise, he would think you crazy if you suggested that he bid farewell to such a pleasant and reasonable existence to join a communistic institution (for all monastic institutions are founded upon the sharing of both wealth and poverty)—never to kiss a girl, never to sit together with a lot of other good fellows and enjoy the simple pleasure of feeling one of them, and to get up at unearthly hours, sleep in an uncomfortable bed, have only one suit of clothes, and spend eighteen hours of each day in prayer and meditation. As a good American, that boy wants to function, and sitting in a dimly lighted chapel, doing good to the souls of other people whom he has never even seen, is not his idea of a really happy existence. And so, unless he was born into a family where medieval traditions still survive, or unless he is just "different" (and that can happen in even a well-regulated family), he will continue most cheerfully and even eagerly to be part of the glamorous adventure that life in America can and should be.

But what of little Caius Theodosius Volutulus, who was born in Rome in the same year, 410, that Alaric plundered Rome? His father had been slain by the barbarians and his mother had fled to their little country house in the Apennines (all that remained to her of her husband's former vast wealth). Under normal circumstances he should have been brought up to play a role in politics and maybe become a senator or even a great general and a governor of some rich province. Now he could look forward to nothing better than a dull and precarious existence in a mountain village where he had to listen all day long to the regrets and the prayers of his dear mamma, who could never get over the terrible fate that had struck her and her deserving family.

If he happened to be a boy of exceptional energy, he might decide to leave home as soon as possible and strike out for himself, even taking service with those half savages who now lorded it over the country that once upon a time had been the heritage of all freeborn Romans. But he was very apt not to be of a robust nature, for his family, accustomed for too long a period of time to a life of ease and plenty, of unearned money and slaves, had sadly petered out. And if he was at the same time endowed with a vague longing for a life of leisure and a polite indulgence in the arts (as is the case with so many slightly decadent children in an ineffectual way), then the prospect of withdrawing from a world which no longer offered him anything he really liked had a great many attractions. And in the case of his sister or a young female relative who had to choose between marrying some dreadful foreigner (who was only the more absurd because he tried so terribly hard to be like a true Roman gentleman) and being raped by an evil-smelling Goth or Vandal soldier who might choose her as part of his own plunder after he had murdered the rest of her family, the temptation to bid farewell to the world and find safety and solace behind the protecting walls of a nunnery was, of course, even stronger.

In the Eastern part of the Roman Empire, the unhealthy conditions of which I have already tried to describe, this desire to escape from a normal existence had made itself felt at a very early date. But there it had taken forms which might be suitable to the Oriental mind but which filled the hearts of the Western Romans, trained for centuries in habits of personal neatness and well-established households, with disgust and contempt. To spend the rest of one's days alone in a filthy cave or perched perilously on the top of a pillar of some ancient temple or withdrawn altogether into the heart of the scorching desert might seem an attractive prospect to a Greek from the shores of some now half-deserted seaport in Asia Minor or from the outskirts of an Egyptian town where the animals fared better than their human keepers; but that would never have done for a Roman boy or girl who had been brought up among the ruins of the old public baths and who had to wash his tunic, if it were his only one, at least twice a month.

Quite naturally, therefore, the monastic development in the West was bound to be entirely different from that in the East, where, until recently, one could still study it in all its less attractive aspects in such aggregations of holy men as lived on the tops of the rocks of Mount Athos in northern Greece or in some of the pre-Bolshevik monasteries of the old Russia.

The very type of man who gave monasticism its first great impetus in Italy indicates how far in this, as in practically all other matters connected with the Church, the western part of the Mediterranean had already grown away from the eastern half. Benedict was born into an aristocratic family that hailed from the province of Umbria. He saw the light of day (just as did the imaginary young man I described a moment ago) during the period when Rome suffered its greatest mortification. The court had left it almost a hundred years before and had found a refuge in the city of Ravenna, which was cut off from the mainland by dismal swamps that kept the enemy at a distance but were just as apt to kill the inhabitants of the city by way of that malaria which afterwards (because of the neglect of the Campagna) turned Rome into one of the most unhealthful cities of the Middle Ages.

And what could a bright and energetic lad find to do in a world that was rapidly degenerating into complete chaos—especially this serious-minded young man who had fallen under the spell of the new teaching? For a short while he attended one of the few remaining schools in Rome; but conditions there were appalling, as they are likely to be in a country where the old social order still vaguely survives, but mostly on its reputation, and where foreign elements (without any tradition of their own) have got into power. When that happens, the older elements are out of luck, for the new arrivals will reduce everything to their own level, which is the normal level for them though not for any of the others, who, however, have no choice, since their very existence has come to depend upon the bounty and good will of the new masters of the state.

All this had happened before, but never on so large a scale or on so radical a basis. I have watched it in a great many countries, and it is not a pretty sight. Most frightening is the rapidity with which the old order will deteriorate until the last vestiges of its former glory are carried to the Flea Market and are there left to rot and rust away because there is no one who any longer has the slightest interest in them. The plight of the older people is pretty sad, but after a few years of dignified silence they quietly betake themselves to the family plot in a neglected cemetery, and their troubles are over. But what is the younger generation going to do? Brought up in the antici-pation of playing some kind of role in a world which their elders prepared for them, they now discover that that world no longer exists, and they are as much at a loss about what to do with themselves as so many canary birds who are suddenly turned loose and told to shift for themselves.

They decide to make the best of their unfortunate bargain, and somehow to make a go of it. They are willing to try their hand at anything that will keep them alive and will show the stuff they are made of. They drop their titles and try to hide a kind of natural elegance that was their birthright. But soon they discover that it is just as difficult to play the proletarian if you have been born the aristocrat as the other way around, and so their coats grow shabbier, and their hope for the future grows dimmer, and they become that most deplorable of all kinds of human beings—people who have come to realize that they are entirely superfluous.

When that point has been reached, they are lost. It is diffi-cult to find out what becomes of them. A few—a very few—will accept favors from the new masters, even to the humblest kind of job, though they will consider such a step a betrayal of their old loyalties. As for the others, they seem to disappear like the paper clips you left around on the porch last fall. Come spring, they are gone, and only a little brown smooch remains to tell you they were ever there. Sometimes, years later, you suddenly meet a ragged figure, but unmistakably a lady or a gentleman, and there is something familiar about the face or the walk. The figure, however, shows no desire to be recog-nized and dissolves itself into a haze of anonymity. Then you write home, "Last Friday I am sure I saw so-and-so. She looked terrible and hastened into a side street. I went to the police and tried to discover her address, but she must have changed her name, for we could find nothing. Too bad! She was a charming person, but that, I suppose, is the way it goes after a revolution."

But in one respect the young man of good family and inherited ability of the days of Rome's great humiliation was better off than his counterpart of the beginning of the twentieth century. There was one field of activity left that was always open to suitable recruits. That was the Church. Having successfully weathered the persecutions of the first three centuries, it was now industriously picking up the remnants of the once-centralized imperial authority. There were several precedents for the new organization, for clericalism as such was nothing new in Rome.

The old Romans, be it remembered, had always believed in religious freedom for their subject peoples. Everybody could find salvation after his own fashion. Even the Jews with their (to the rest of the world) rather absurd system of eating and drinking and doing almost everything differently from the way it was done by their neighbors had been allowed complete freedom of worship. There had been trouble about letting the Roman legionaries in Palestine carry banners with the picture of the emperor on them, but in the end the Romans had merely shrugged their shoulders. People so fanatical about their own religious observances that they refused to fight on the Sabbath, even in defense of their own holy city—well, they were just beyond human understanding, but, since they closely stuck to themselves and made no effort to convert others to their own queer way of thinking and were industrious and frugal citizens, it was good policy to leave them alone and tax them to the limit.

But for the rest, everybody could pretty well think what he pleased, and one foreign goddess had been established for so many years and enjoyed such wide popularity that she had become the center of a religious cult which centuries before the arrival of Christianity had developed into an organization so exactly like the papacy that the latter may well have chosen it as its model.

Isis was a goddess who had become enormously popular all through the valley of the Nile during the twelfth century B.C. She gradually became to the people of the whole eastern part of the Mediterranean what the Madonna was to be to the people of Europe in the Middle Ages. She had her own priests and choir singers and monks, and at the head of her organization was a high priest who was just like a pope. Regular daily services were held in all her temples and a sort of mass was read by white-robed priests who were tonsured like the Christian priests of today. Therefore, it was comparatively easy for the bishop of Rome to build up a structure of his own, patterned after that of his most dangerous enemy, the Egyptian goddess Isis, who was so obstinate a rival that the last of her temples were not closed until the middle of the sixth century.

This is not supposed to be a book of history, and therefore I cannot go into the details of the fascinating history of how the bishop of Rome (in the beginning merely one of a hundred or so bishops, some of them living in more important cities than he did) gradually got himself recognized as the head of the whole Western Church. The development was quite like that of the Roman state itself. But when I have said that, I have told you exactly nothing at all. For though there are probably a hundred thousand books that have been written about the history of Rome—and there well may be another hundred thousand—we always come back to the same question nobody thus far has successfully answered: why should an obscure little village on a miserable little river in a part of the world that was then on the outskirts of the civilized world ever have become the center of an empire that eventually was to rule the entire civilized Occident?

There have been all sorts of guesses, hypotheses, and suggestions, but none of them quite covers the case. The economists (who now rule the historical roost) point to the fact that Rome arose where the Tiber was easily fordable and, being situated on a road between the northern and southern parts of the Italian peninsula, could not have helped but grow into an important commercial center. What of it? All sorts of other villages have since time immemorial been located at such convenient places, and they have never got anywhere at all. Others have claimed that the warriorlike qualities of the old Romans gave them what it takes to achieve a world empire. Other tribes just as warriorlike, or perhaps even more so, fought just as bravely, started upon just as many expeditions, slaughtered just as many enemies, and never accomplished a thing. And in the case of the Romans, we cannot even pretend that they were brighter and more imaginative than their neighbors, for they were not. The Greeks were a thousand times brighter, and the Phoenicians, who founded their colony of Carthage at the most strategic parts of the Mediterranean—Carthage and Marseille—displayed a much greater insight into the future.

Then what was it? I have a guess, but it is not a popular one, and I give it for what it is worth. There is such a thing in this world as genius. We don't know what it is, but, like electricity (about whose essence we likewise know little), we know how it works, for that we can see. Now, occasionally it will happen that in some clan which thus far has never shown signs of any particular brilliancy there will arise a person or a family of extraordinary ability in some particular field of endeavor. A Veit Bach comes along, and the world benefits from the presence of literally dozens of outstanding musicians descended from him. We have thus far paid very little attention to the history of some families of genius. We feel that there is something undemocratic about paying too much attention to the exceptional man, for this is supposed to be the age of the average man, and what he can't do nobody really has any right to do. All the same, history is there to bear me out: it is still the exceptional individual who dominates the landscape, and if he combines with the right kind of woman (which he does very rarely), the results may mean a political or social or artistic or scientific flare-up which will be seen for a long time far and wide.

We do not know altogether how the laws of heredity work—in fact, they often seem to go their own sweet way. But if all of us in this world are more or less related (and rather closely too), then it follows that in a small town or village the inter-relationship will be even greater and that curious quality or characteristic—call it what you want—which, for lack of a better word, we define as genius has an excellent chance to become the specialty of that particular neighborhood.

In the case of the people who, during the eight centuries before our era, were settling in the plain of Latium, this genius expressed itself in an ability to fight, combined with a pronounced gift for administration. This fighting ability was common enough among all prehistoric tribes of five thousand years ago (or, for that matter, of today), but few of them have known how to keep what they had got without destroying the inner spirit of their subjects to such an extent that, instead of becoming willing allies, they developed into bitter and irreconcilable enemies. The Nazis are a gruesome example of what will happen when the destructive genius of a race is not offset by a corresponding talent for constructive work. God knows, Caius Julius Caesar was no angel. After he had subdued a rebellious Germanic tribe, he could behave with the callous cruelty of a Nazi general let loose among the Poles or the Ukrainians. But as soon as the last of his wholesale executions had come to an end and the last of the victims had been buried, the chapter of destruction was closed, and on a fresh page there appeared a number of items designed to put his newly acquired province on its feet and give it some of the benefits of having become part of a well-organized and smoothly administered empire. And that extraordinary talent for exercising authority without making those who had been forced to submit to this authority too painfully conscious of the fact that they were no longer masters of their own fate— it was that which set the Romans apart from all the other conquering races of the old world. For force alone is helpless when a people aspires to become a colonial power. Unless the administrators be natural psychologists with an unconscious feeling for what to do and what not to do (sometimes under very difficult circumstances), they will never get anywhere at all.

Unfortunately, or rather fortunately, that is not something which can be learned from textbooks. Good textbooks will help, just as good textbooks will allow the average human being to develop into a fairly competent doctor, though only by an act of God can he become a healer. But once more I am losing myself in a maze of speculation about subjects of which we are still in deep and dark ignorance. The muse of history, being a woman, loves to treat us to interesting dishes of her own making, but when we find them interesting to the palate and say, "Please, lady, how did you do it? What did you put into it and how long did you keep it in the oven?" she smiles pleasantly, but, like a good cook, never betrays her secrets, and we are no wiser than we were before.

Therefore, all I can say now (leaving it to my much wiser great-great-grandchildren to contradict me) is that in a particular spot at the foot of the Sabine mountains there arose a village in which a gift for war, combined with administrative abilities of a most pronounced sort, made itself so manifest that, without at first any definite plans for world conquest, it eventually became the center of the ancient classical world. And Rome's genius for administration proved so strong that it continued to function long after it had lost any large political significance. By which I do not mean that every Roman was a

Chapter VIII

Caesar or an Augustus. Most Romans were as commonplace in their appearance and behavior as any modern British or Dutch colonial official. Occasionally they also turned crook and oppressed those entrusted to their care, but by and large they did an efficient if somewhat unimaginative job. And even after the outstanding figures among them had begun to disappear, the old spirit continued. For the pattern had been set, and once any kind of social or intellectual pattern has been definitely set, it will maintain itself in spite of everything.

In this such patterns remind me of our landscapes or our cities. Wherever I have gone I have always been impressed by the indestructibility of the earliest impress the human hand made upon the natural background of either mountains or plains or human settlements. Of course, you have got to learn those signs before you can easily read them, just as a geologist has to be familiar with the rudiments of his science before he can tell you by what original process a formation came into being. But that knowledge is something you can pick up easily enough if you are interested, and it will pay you for your troubles. For even a superficial examination will show you that a city you always held to be of medieval origin is actually much older, and developed out of a prehistoric settlement, while a rococo town will in turn betray that it is nothing but an overgrown medieval village.

Ancient Roman fortresses too, no matter how often they have been overrun by hostile hordes or how frequently they have been reduced to ashes, will still give evidence of their having been very much alive. The same holds good for roads that often have not been used for a thousand years. The airplane has been of great service to us in this business of reconstructing our bygone world, for the surface of the earth as seen from a great elevation clearly betrays every secret of its long-forgotten past. And the same holds good for those living organisms we call nations. Their original talent for some particular

form of human endeavor, whether administering foreign territories, painting pictures, writing symphonies, losing themselves in religious speculation, being a constant nuisance and
menace to their neighbors, cooking, fiddling, or exploring the
oceans, will continue to manifest itself for centuries after the
time they were at the top of their development.

Of course, conditions may arise that will put a definite end
to this original talent, just as a site may be so completely destroyed by an earthquake or a flood that it is changed into
something entirely different. The Greeks may be so completely
overrun by an endless succession of barbarous invaders—Germanic tribes from the north, Saracen conquerors from the east,
Caucasians from the west—that in the end the Greek blood
will have become so hopelessly diluted that it will have practically ceased to exist. The Italian peninsula may have suffered
so many foreign conquests—it may have been plundered by
successive bands of Goths, Vandals, Longobards, Alemains,
Norsemen, Frenchmen, Spaniards, and medieval Germans—
that finally the old blood will have become completely wiped
out, and nothing will remain but a name. In that case, we cannot predict what will happen, for even the original language
may disappear and be replaced by another one, as happened in
Bulgaria. But unless there is that kind of brutal interference
with the normal development of a nation, it will remain faithful to its earliest pattern for an astonishingly long period of
time, and we can observe this in the city of the Seven Hills.
After it had ceased to be the civic ruler of the world and had
become a mere shadow of its former self, a poverty-stricken collection of hovels inhabited by a mere handful of sick and
ragged men and women instead of the million that it had held
within its walls during the old imperial days, it was able to
carry on as the generally recognized spiritual head of its former
domains. And every Roman youngster who formerly had ex-

pected to enter the service of the state now looked forward to a career in the Church.

We had a similar development in Germany and Austria after World War I. The younger sons of the old nobility were deprived of a chance to enter the army and the civil service. They had always been good at that sort of work, but the army and the civil service had all but ceased to exist. They were good routine men and had a decided gift for jobs that demanded a meticulous observance of bureaucratic details. They gave up their former dream of wearing a uniform and got themselves ordinary business suits, and instead of working in a *Kriegsministerium* as a clerk with spurs, they hired themselves out to the *Farben* Syndicate or the Coal Cartel or Herr Krupp's steel works or the champagne industry, and in the evening they put on a dress suit and haunted the night clubs where the figures of high finance found relaxation from the exertions of the day.

Well, there you have, in a general way, the Rome of the early days of the Church. Since the Church was the only organization that offered a bright and energetic young man that chance to function for which he had been "conditioned" (as modern psychology calls it), he entered the Church.

There were, of course, those who were actuated by higher motives—who had heard the call and obeyed it. But the rank and file, while no doubt good Christians, were also of an essentially practical mind and took to a clerical career because it offered the only chance to function as all Romans of the higher classes had functioned for over a thousand years.

This has been a pretty long detour, but I have always felt the desire to express my opinion about a matter usually explained in somewhat different terms, and this was my chance. Whereupon, with apologies to the reader (who, however, may have found something of interest in this), I go back to Saint

Benedict of Nursia, who offered me this welcome excuse to have my say upon the still mysterious problem of why Rome so easily and so naturally developed into the capital of Christianity, and who (though quite unconsciously) exercised such a great influence upon the early history of my own part of the world.

Benedict noticed the increase in the monastic fever and, being an orderly-minded Roman citizen, he cannot possibly have liked what he saw. Unless this enthusiasm for a solitary and ascetic life were severed from chaos and anarchism among its devotees, it would never get anywhere at all. It had to be firmly taken in hand by an energetic leader and had to be reorganized after the practical imperial Roman pattern or it would lead to absurd excesses, and in that case would do the Church more harm than good.

Hence the new rules that were laid down for those who wished to escape from our turbulent world and who wanted to prepare their souls in silence and seclusion for the great adventure of the life that lay beyond death. Saint Benedict came by them the hard way. Disgusted with the world around him, he had fled into the wilderness of the Abruzzi, where, in the shadow of one of Nero's old villas, he found a convenient cave. Other hermits attached to this neighborhood asked him to organize them into a monastic group and to become their head. He accepted this dignity, but when he tried to enforce a little discipline in this motley group of holy men, they tried to poison him, which clearly shows from among what kind of people the monks were recruited during the first quarter of the sixth century. Back he went to his lonely cave, but again his colleagues asked him to become their leader, and this time he laid down a definite set of rules for their behavior. This time it worked. Twelve small monasteries were established, and when local rivalry forced him to give up his abode among the Abruzzi mountains, he himself withdrew to a steep hill between Rome and Naples. There, at Monte Cassino, he built himself a new home which soon was to become the center of the monastic movement for the whole Western world.

Many other monastic orders were founded during the next seven hundred years, and they varied in a great many details, but it was Saint Benedict who had so successfully laid down the general outline for this kind of work that all subsequent organizations of the nature were patterned after the great experiment at Monte Cassino.

Saint Benedict insisted upon an intelligent but severe discipline for all members of a monastic group—a discipline that involved hard physical and mental labor. One either earned one's keep or one stayed out. Spiritual self-indulgence was not tolerated. The odor of unwashed bodies was not in itself considered a guarantee of sanctity, and indeed was frowned upon.

The Middle Ages, with their execrable housing facilities, are symbolized by unwashed bodies; and the lack of safety of the times, which forced people to flock together in messy little city streets without any care for public health, made it difficult for anyone to observe the personal cleanliness that had been a characteristic of the Greeks and the Romans. And the disapproval in which the Church held all sorts of physical exercises (since pride of the body might mean a corresponding contempt for the soul) had led to the complete disappearance of sport.

This attitude may also have been somewhat colored by the hatred the Christians of the third and fourth centuries felt for the stadiums and colosseums and circuses which were part of the architectural plan of every ancient city. Not so very long before they had been used for the favorite sport of the bestial mob of imperial Rome, which, just as a modern Spanish crowd gathers together to see a drab bull being tortured, had derived immense satisfaction in seeing Christian men and women and children being burned like so many human beacons or being thrown to the wild animals. Sport, therefore, in the eyes of the people of the second and third centuries, had become identified with cruelty, and one can hardly blame the Fathers for their intense hatred of anything that reminded them of the days of the Church's suffering and humiliation. Therefore our ancestors of the Middle Ages paid very little attention to that physical hygiene which today has become almost a fetish. Cities were vast garbage cans and the happy breeding places of every sort and variety of microbe.

The monasteries, however, were far ahead of the civic communities of their own day. They maintained a semblance of public cleanliness and as a result were apt to escape many of the epidemics which swept over Europe with the rapidity of forest fires and often killed one third or even one half of the population. All of which has made me completely revise the opinion I held in my youth, when, because of my Calvinistic upbringing, a monk seemed no better than a loafer and a social parasite. He undoubtedly became just that, but at a much later date, and originally he had performed a most useful task. For if the earliest missionaries (who got all the glory and most of the saintships) were the shock troops and parachutists of the great Christian assault upon the uncivilized tribes of northern Europe, then (to continue this very modern metaphor) the monks were the infantrymen who have got to do the marching and the mopping up, the building of the roads and bridges, and the setting up of a civil government in the midst of the ruined villages and towns, and who have to live a grubby existence, full of endless hours of boredom and routine, while the shock troops march forward and get the applause, the medals and flowers, and the girls.

This has been quite a long chapter, and I have wandered far, but if I want to understand not merely who I am but how I came to be the way I am, then I have to dig deep into those formative years when the people who begot me entirely changed their ways of living and thinking. This happened in the seventh and eighth centuries, when they were exposed to a new philosophy of life and habits of living and became members of the new world empire—the empire of the spirit of the Christian Church.

Some centuries afterwards, when the monks had long ceased to be the living symbols of that message of love and humanity which Christ had brought to our world and when the monastic establishments had become a terrific drain upon the public exchequer without rendering any kind of service in return for their bed and board, in countries that became predominantly Protestant the Reformation turned upon these institutions with such a deep-seated hatred that vast numbers of them were wiped out. Even the early Christians had not done such a thorough job when destroying the old pagan temples. Those churches which could be converted into Protestant houses of prayer were allowed to survive, though they were despoiled of all their former luxury and appeal to the eye. I know this because I never saw a nunnery or a monastery until I was twelve or thirteen years old and made my first trip down the Rhine, and then I looked at them with grave suspicion as places where the Inquisition was probably still engaged in torturing innocent little old women who had been caught reading their Bibles in a Dutch translation.

I found cities and villages on the maps of my atlas, the names of which clearly betrayed their monastic origin, and I knew that we lived amongst the ruins of several old monastic holdings. But it is only recently, during the great Roman Catholic revival of the last twenty years, that monasteries have come back to the Low Countries and, just as in the eastern part of our republic, Roman Catholics are buying up all the best pieces of real estate and are making a bold and at times arrogant bid for a supremacy to which—numerically speaking, at least—they are by no means entitled. In the eighties of the last century, that was not yet true. The Kingdom of the Netherlands, as far as I know, had merely followed the example of Switzerland, where, since the year 1848, all monastic establishments have been positively forbidden and where the Jesuits, in their quality of Jesuits, have never been allowed to make a public appearance and are only tolerated as short-term visitors. The country would have saved itself a lot of trouble if it had followed the Swiss example, for the moment clericalism becomes a political issue (and let six Jesuits come together for five minutes in the name of pugnacious old Don Ignacio and you will have a clerical problem on your hands in six minutes), there is an end to all national peace and harmony.

But it is now too late, and, unless the horrors of the Nazi usurpation are changing all that, I can see little hope for the immediate future. The Church offers too many opportunities for little men of vast ambitions not to be exceedingly popular among the lower middle classes, and the future in this respect is far from bright, for the liberals of the middle of the last century (and what a magnificent group they were!) are rapidly dying out, and their lukewarm successors are so caught up in sentimental nonsense about equal rights for all that they would surrender the country to any party strongly enough organized to gain a majority at the elections.

Equal rights constitute a fine ideal, but somehow or other it seems to work only under very limited circumstances. Of course, the modern Swiss are as progressive and well run a nation as any that existed before the Hitler deluge. You could do as you pleased and think as you pleased, but, being very sober-minded realists, they knew that this state of absolute social and intellectual and spiritual freedom would come to an end the moment you extended equal rights to troublemakers. Clericals in general and the Jesuits in particular had been troublemakers ever since they had been given complete liberty of action in the Swiss Republic. Early in the forties of the last century the canton of Lucerne called in the Jesuits to teach in their public schools. In the year 1843 some Catholic cantons secretly formed a Sonderbund of their own—a country, so to speak, within a country—which undoubtedly would have come under Jesuit control. The Swiss Diet, by a large majority, then declared the formation of the Sonderbund unconstitutional and ordered its dissolution. The Sonderbund refused to comply, having already made an appeal to Metternich, the Austrian chancellor and the leader of the European reaction, and to Guizot, who had given up his old liberal principles (he had started out in life as a historian) and who had become one of the mainstays of the more and more conservative policies of King Louis-Philippe. Lord Palmerston let it be known that he would support the Diet, but England was far away and would hardly risk a European war for a few Swiss cantons of which it knew nothing except that they were a nice place in which to spend the summer, with neat bedrooms and comparatively honest landlords.

The problem, however, was settled in short order by the mobilization of the then (as now) highly efficient Swiss army. A general named Dufour, whose parents hailed from the Calvinistic Republic of Geneva (the only Swiss canton that had always insisted on calling itself a republic)—a veteran of the Emperor Napoleon's artillery, a former teacher of Napoleon III during the latter's exile in Switzerland, and the future presiding officer of the international conference that framed the Geneva Convention which in the year 1864 gave us the Red Cross—made short shrift of the Sonderbund army and by his wise moderation prevented the outbreak of a regular civil war. But the new Federal Constitution of the year 1848 leaned heavily upon the Constitution of the United States of America, and the liberals who were in control of the legislature established a maximum of personal freedom while taking all the necessary precautions against the recurrence of deplorable events like those of the year 1843 and making impossible the re-establishment of any kind of Sonderbund.

But Swiss fear of further clerical meddling found an even more considered expression in a new Federal Constitution of the year 1874, and once again it was affirmed that the Swiss Republic, come what might, intended to protect its peaceful, harmonious domestic arrangements against all clerical encroachment. Ever since, the Federal government has most carefully enforced this rule: freedom and equality of action can be accorded only to those who from their side have given evidence of a certain willingness to play the game according to the rules.

The Kingdom of the Netherlands failed to take this precaution, and the political squabbles of the last hundred years and the methods used by the Church to regain its former powers and prerogatives are (to express myself with unusual moderation) not exactly inspiring. But all that (and I shall have a lot more to say about it in a second volume) does not change the fact that this same Church, when it was young and the physical and spiritual representative of a magnificent new ideal, did more than any other agency to bring my ancestors of a thousand years ago within the pale of civilization. For once those benighted heathen had accepted the new God (whom to a certain extent they continued to identify with their old Wotan) and had ceased to slaughter such missionaries as fell into their hands—roughly speaking, in the eighth and ninth centuries of our era—they soon realized that they had done themselves a mighty good turn.

At first the asceticism of the monks and the frugality of their way of living did not greatly appeal to the northern people, but it was a way of living so compatible with the needs of the average Italian that even today ninety-nine per cent of the Italian people ask for very little more than what a monk gets —a little bread, a few onions, some garlic, very little meat, and a few glasses of a very sober wine. The Church, which was a practical institution, realized this and, except for a few feast days when these barbarians were not allowed to guzzle and a hint that drinking to excess was not exactly compatible with a true Christian existence, few efforts were made to interfere with their diet. It is curious to observe what a nation will stand if the authorities do not interfere too severely with its eating and drinking habits, and how it will rise in revolt the moment it is urged to take better care of its health (a losing battle once waged by Mr. Thomas Jefferson of Albemarle County, Virginia, who wasted a great deal of his valuable time trying to change his fellow citizens from drunken whisky swillers into moderate wine drinkers and to pry them loose from that everlasting frying pan and teach them the charms of the grill).

And what of the other benefits? It is difficult for us in the year 1944 to understand how primitive the conditions still were in those countries which, until the arrival of Herr Hitler's New Order, were the undisputed leaders of what we usually call "progress."

Here is a small example of what I was thinking while writing this. The monks gave the people among whom they settled their first notions of the use of the calendar. The ancient Germans had known the difference between night and day and had observed the regular sequence of the seasons. It was long before the invention of clocks, and those printed calendars with which your laundryman and your tailor favor you at Christmastime were not yet known. The obliging monks hung bells in their towers with which to remind the folk who lived within listening distance that it was time to get up for their morning prayers, time to go to work, time for vespers, time to go to Mass, time to do this and do that. Likewise, the necessity of fixing Easter for every coming year made people conscious of the fact that there were such sciences as astronomy and mathematics, for without their assistance one could hardly have discovered which was the Sunday after the full moon after the vernal equinox (unless the full moon came on a Sunday, in which case Easter was observed one week later).

I am still a pagan when it comes to this feast, which my earliest ancestors associated with their goddess of the spring. I think that it is one of the pleasantest seasons of the year, and, as I am not a churchgoer, the fact that the early Christians identified it with the Passion and Resurrection of their Lord and celebrated it with a week of mournful faces and costumes does not very greatly affect me. But this public holiday, which may come any time from February to April, has always struck me as somewhat of an absurdity. However, I should remember that this arrangement was decided upon by that Council of Nicaea of the year 325, which did everything according to the rule that was afterwards to contribute so much to the glory of the Austrian Empire—the rule that asked, "Why should we do things simply when we can just as easily do them in a complicated fashion?" And as the people of the early Middle Ages had a great deal of spare time on their hands, they probably never gave the matter a thought, but lived happily and contentedly according to that calendar which their new masters had laid down for them. However, it was a decided step forward, as they now observed a calendar that was international and no longer a purely local affair.

But there were ever so many other improvements in their daily lives which were the direct result of their having accepted this new God and which made themselves felt as time went by. I have already mentioned the practical aspects of the conquest of northern Europe by people who in the beginning at least were almost exclusively recruited from among men who had been exposed to a higher degree of civilization than had thus far penetrated into this wilderness. Better agricultural methods were introduced. Better crops and a better breed of cattle were the immediate result and set the inhabitants free from the everlasting specter of hunger. Housing was not yet improved. My grandfathers of that day continued to live peacefully in their hovels in the close companionship of their hogs and calves, but in some parts of the country, for that matter, they continued to do so until the early years of my own youth. And why not? They realized that this close proximity of human beings and animals does not exactly make for that clean atmosphere of which we make such a fetish in our modern world of high hygienic standards. But when you explained this to them (as I sometimes tried to do), they would answer: "Well, we have heard about lots of people who were frozen to death, but never yet of one who was stunk to death. So why should we worry?"

I very much doubt that, during the first few hundred years at least after their arrival, the monks were able to make any dent in the general ignorance of the people. The early Middle Ages (and the later ones too) still regarded an ability to read and write as something little needed by a gentleman. All through history we can observe definite styles in that which is considered "fashionable" and that which is not. A medieval king at an official banquet would gorge his guest and would encourage him to "please have another helping of this chicken. It is remarkably good and greasy!" with an eagerness which is now regarded as an expression of hopeless middle-class vulgarity. King Louis XIV of France could afford to take an active part in a ballet amidst the hearty plaudits of his courtiers, but can anyone think of a president of the United States doing a little *pas seul* with the Russian ballet without losing all chances of ever being re-elected? Hardly. But he can play poker with his cronies and sing barbershop ballads with his pals in the East Room and, except for the stricter church folk, nobody will take great offense at it, for it merely shows that he is a simple-hearted, democratic fellow who does not feel that he has grown too good for the rest of the boys.

The Middle Ages were dominated by the belief that there was something magic about the written word and that it should therefore be left to clerics who had learned how to protect themselves against the evil inherent in a page of those cabalistic signs. When I was reporting the Russian revolution of 1906 for the Associated Press, I came upon cases of peasants who had drowned all the books they had found in the country houses they had marked down for plunder and the torch. For they had a deep hatred for every printed volume. By means of the knowledge their former masters had derived from these accursed books, they had turned themselves into those superior beings who for so many centuries had been able to keep the peasants in their place. Therefore, let the books perish first of all. Then the spell would be broken and the peasant would be the noble's equal.

Some such idea seems to have prevailed throughout the Middle Ages, and the only place where it was safe to occupy oneself with reading and writing was behind the high protecting walls of a monastery. Many of the monks were sadly lacking in learning. The brighter ones among them were forever complaining of the ignorance of most of their colleagues. Even so, they were in literary matters at least a thousand times superior to almost every knight, and we should be grateful to them for having preserved some semblance of learning during an age when the average layman had as much respect for a beautifully illuminated copy of Aristotle's *De anima* as a Nazi lout now feels for a rare copy of a twelfth-century Talmud.

But then again, the Middle Ages, which were much more practical and earthy-minded than we usually believe, soon discovered that this familiarity with the written word had also its practical side. It could be used for keeping birth, marriage, and death records. A last will and testament now became a document (carefully filed away in the abbot's iron chest) instead of a mere oral agreement. A community that was becoming more and more agricultural needed a system by which all people at all times could know exactly where their own property ended and their neighbors' began.

But aside from these purely practical innovations, the new priesthood (for many of the monks were also ordained priests) introduced new conceptions about the right and righteous way of living which were of tremendous importance. Many of these conceptions survived a sufficient number of centuries for my own little philosophy of life to have been influenced by them —even if unconsciously.

When the plains and mountains of northern Europe were at last settled, the wanderers who had occupied this empty territory became like our own pioneers of a hundred years ago. The gods they brought with them we know—as a rule—only by way of Herr Richard Wagner's operas. But Wagner, who lived in a stuffy world of ornamental gas chandeliers and who composed even his most ferocious music in dressing gowns that were combinations of silk and velvet, succeeded in giving his Valhalla an air of middle-class complacency. His Wotans and Brunhilds and Siegfrieds and Sieglindes remained German operatic bassos, tenors, and sopranos, and you are always conscious that right after the performance they will go to a near-by (and not quite first-class) restaurant where they will partake of a *sauer Häring* and that afterwards they will retire to Frau Schmaltz's elegant boardinghouse, where they will have boiled eggs for breakfast (a second one being a pfennig extra).

Then, during the middle of the last century (under the impetus of the glorious victories of the Franco-Prussian War), a number of German *Schriftsteller* (a word which for one reason or another I have always detested) started a school of writing that tried to depict these heavenly heroes as if they had been the commanders of so many Prussian regiments, goose-stepping heavily in the general direction of the palace of Versailles, that justice might be done and the shame of the endless Napoleonic victories might at last be wiped out.

I read all those books when I was young, for they were almost all one could get, with the exception of *The Three Musketeers* (which was thought to be a little too immoral for our youthful tastes), Sir Walter Scott (then beginning to be pretty heavy going, with the exception of *Ivanhoe*), and Jules Verne, who was safe but who might prove to be too exciting for our placid Dutch imagination.

I never liked those early gods of my fathers, finding them as objectionable as some of the German businessmen my father would sometimes bring home for dinner—men with fine crops of whiskers and smelling of beer. Because of these early influences, I have never been able quite to understand what these gods must have meant to the people who worshiped them. I experience no such difficulty in the case of the Greek gods. It is quite easy for me to see the world around me as the home of a number of lesser deities who are never seen but whose presence is just as real as that of the nimble woodchuck who these last two years seems to have lived under our garage and who is a most welcome guest, even if occasionally his insatiable appetite makes him eat something he should have left alone.

I know for a certainty that Pan has long since left Arcadia and has come to live in Connecticut, and that he spends part of every spring bathing in the warm springs that are said to exist in the more impenetrable part of that most welcome Tod's Point wilderness which lies right outside of my window, at the other side of Greenwich Cove. Indeed, one of my main objections to having Tod's Point converted into a public playground is the sure knowledge that Pan will then move farther inland. The old Greek gods were fastidious creatures and avoided crowds as carefully as I do. But if they knew that you respected their privacy, they would become the most amiable and delightful of acquaintances. For a few flowers or some other token of appreciation of their presence they would render you all kinds of little services—bring Mungo home when he had wandered off too far, keep your garden fresh during a drought, pull a skunk out of the way just before Jimmie. calling it a "nice kitten," had tried to pick it up and bring it home. And sometimes, very late at night and with the moon shining brightly, they would bring their girl friends around for a swim from Edwin Lucas's dock and then, provided you were not too brash about it, you would see sights of such utter loveliness that you wished you had lived twenty-five centuries ago when an occasional mortal still had a chance to qualify for membership among the immortal gods.

But never for a moment have I had the slightest desire to spend even a single afternoon in that dark habitat of our Norse gods who, cheerful creatures, called the place where they held their meetings the Hall of the Slain. For the crowd there must have resembled nothing quite so much as the Munich Beer Hall where Hitler and his cronies swilled their *Spatenbräu* (on borrowed money) in the days before they came to power and where they laid plans for the glorious return of Wotan and his boozy paladins.

I have observed the Nazis—the nearest return to the primitive Teutonic *Ur-Mensch*—in sobriety and in alcohol, and from a careful study of this species of subhuman brutes I have come to the regrettable conclusion that the wrong people won the battle of the Teutoburger Wald, here and there he may have had his moments of a kind of somber beauty which I thought I could hear in the music of Wagner, who (all this is pure guesswork on my part, and I may be entirely wrong) may have caught the old German spirit when he expressed himself in his melodies just as he lost it whenever he descended to the use of mere words. But by and large it was a dreadful world—

that world of my ancestors—when first they moved into those swampy regions which were to be their permanent home, and I shall ever marvel at the miracle that was performed when these savages were pried away from their old beliefs, customs, manners, and habits, and were formed into approximately civilized human beings.

Hell's Fire and Why It Was Lighted

THE LAST chapter was much too long, but the foundations of a house are quite as important as that which appears above ground, and I am now going to discuss the second most important step along that line of development which has made me what I am today.

The first step took place during the glacial periods when the human race was confronted with the choice of either learning a lot of things in a very short period of time or perishing. Choosing to learn, by a sudden impetus it acquired much useful new information and survived. The second step came tens of thousands of years later when my ancestors were given the basis of a philosophy of life which went completely contrary to the old laws of the jungle and which insisted that every man was every other man's brother and that he should treat him as a friend instead of an enemy. I said a moment ago that the conversion of the heathen to the Christian faith should be taken as a practical matter—almost a matter of necessity—rather than as a great spiritual urge forward toward a more ethical form of existence. These ethical conceptions existed. They were, however, a by-product and so slow of development that even today they have not yet gone beyond the preliminary stage. But even so, the change from heathendom to Christianity was a tremendous step forward, probably the greatest step forward during all the years we have been on this earth.

It is difficult to say this in the year 1944, after what was supposed to be one of the most enlightened nations of modern times suddenly relapsed into a state of savagery of which even the cavemen would have felt thoroughly ashamed. But the Nazis are merely interrupting the normal development of our civilization, just as any one of us may catch a disease or even temporarily lose his mind and be set back a great many years before he can once more pick up the pieces and continue to work at the useful tasks on which he was engaged.

Between the average individual of pre-Christian days and the average individual of post-Christian days there is a difference so vast that the two can hardly be compared. Yet, in many ways the change was not noticeable. Violence and greed continued to play just as predominant a part in people's lives as they had done before. The crassest forms of superstition continued to enjoy widespread popularity. Even the Church practiced cruelties which are abominations in our eyes, but just the same there was a difference, and if we contemplate that difference from the angle of the ages, then we must confess that by and large it was a change for the good. There had been outstanding people in the ancient world who not only had discovered the existence of conscience in their minds or souls or whatever they wanted to call them, but who also had insisted that everybody was endowed with such a conscience and that everybody should do his best to develop it and let it be his guide in everything he said or did.

But a Socrates had had no chance against the mass mind of his own day and age, and the democracy of Athens had killed him, even as, a few centuries later, the theocracy of Jerusalem was to murder Jesus. There had even been most carefully thought-out philosophical systems which had taught that we should let that still, small, inner voice be our ever-present mentor and let it tell us what to do (and even more, what not to do) in every action we undertook. But they had been like the earliest compasses of the Middle Ages. Only a very few people had been able to get hold of them, and even fewer had known how to handle them successfully. The others had continued to set their course any old way, and most of them had come to grief. For the masses cannot possibly follow a philosophical system which appeals to certain sensitive emotions they do not possess and probably never will acquire so long as we continue to breed for quantity rather than for quality.

Socrates may be said to have suffered for conscience' sake (quite apart from the complicated politics of the situation). And ever since, the man of pure ideas and ideals has suffered a similar fate. For the average man needs something concrete, something he can see and hear and feel in a concrete way, before he will accept its existence. And there is where the Christian missionary of the earliest days of the Middle Ages had his tremendous advantage over all the preachers of the philosophical systems of the days of the Romans and the Greeks. As mere individuals, these Ludgers and Winifreds and Willibrords and Eligiuses who taught the Christian faith to my ancestors were undoubtedly much inferior to a Socrates or an Epicurus, a Zeno or a Democritus. They lacked their learning, their wide understanding of the physical world around them, and their bold curiosity about everything pertaining to the human race. From an ethical point of view, these heathen philosophers lived their lives according to standards that were just as elevated as those of any Christian of the last two thousand years. And if they had been successful in their teaching, we should have had a much better world, for they respected the mortal body just as much as the immortal soul. But they could never hope to attract more than a mere handful of followers, for they talked and taught in terms that were entirely incomprehensible to the average man and woman of their time. Perhaps it would be best to say that they were artists of the soul and that it took a practical craftsman like the Nazarene carpenter to find a way of reaching the masses.

Report to Saint Peter

Kant's categorical imperative might have been just as satisfactory a rule of life as the Sermon on the Mount, but Kant was a professor of metaphysics, mechanics, physical geography, logic, and mineralogy in a provincial little Prussian town, and gained fame by writing a book the first sentence of which is thirty-six pages long (I am quoting from memory), with the verb next to the last word. And he lived a dignified existence and never showed himself to the populace unless his wig were properly powdered and he wore the right kind of stock—a most amiable creature who sincerely loved his fellow men. His private life (except for his almost Voltairian addiction to coffee) was as pure as that of any saint, and everything he ever wrote or said had but one single purpose—to make this earth a happier and more sensible place of abode for all of God's strangely assorted creatures. But Immanuel never could have hoped to reach any of the butchers, bakers, and candlestick-makers who gazed at him and politely lifted their caps when the Herr Professor took that famous daily walk of his by which the townspeople of Königsberg used to set their clocks. He was too far removed from the ordinary mass of humanity to remain anything but an abstract principle.

The world of the ancients had been full of Immanuel Kants, and all glory to them and praise be to the noble efforts they made to humanize the human beast. But their spiritual products had been for only what modern advertising agencies call a "quality market." They had not been suitably packaged for mass consumption and had lacked that personal "we to you" appeal that is absolutely essential if a manufacturer (whether he sells roasted peanuts or ideas) wishes to reach the largest possible number of customers.

But look at those young Frisians and Franks and Saxons who, after a dozen years of training in some southern monastery, were sent back to their old villages in the northern wilderness, there to spread the Good Word among their own folk. There was nothing remote about what they came to tell their former neighbors. Like most primitive people, they were extremely simple, almost childlike, in their reactions towards anything that was brought to their attention. They had no taste for the complicated. It merely annoyed them and upset them and made them feel their own inferiority when they were brought in contact with something they instinctively felt to be of a superior order. They would have shied away from a performance of *Hamlet,* but give them a good Punch and Judy with situations they could understand and they would come back for more day after day, though it would always be the same play, with Death (and the deader Death looked, the more they loved it) forever making a grab at Judy, and Punch arriving just in the nick of time to hammer hell out of Death with a stick so big that it looked like one of the poles of the gallows.

I know whereof I speak. I was an inveterate Punch-and-Judy-goer for some ten years of my life, and we howled with anger whenever the Professor dared to change one single word in that text which had come down to us from the remote obscurity of the early Middle Ages.

Am I indulging in too brutal a mixture of the sublime and the ridiculous? By no means. The two are very closely related anyway, and the younger we are, the better we know this. These people were still very, very young. Indeed, so young that they still believed in fairy stories and what lovelier fairy story than the charming mother and her child—that mother still so happily ignorant of the terrible fate that awaited Him and not realizing in the least that she had given birth to the Son of God and that someday she would share in His glory as the ruler of this earth.

But other religions had offered these benighted heathen that same emotional appeal, and I don't think it was that which would have persuaded my ancestors of the eighth century to accept Christianity as the faith best suited to their needs. They lived in a world of stern realities, and those holy men who spoke unto them were no dreamers. They were men of practical experience who insisted upon practical results and who had all the arguments necessary to obtain them. Some of these arguments lie so far behind us that we have forgotten them, or, whenever reminded of their existence, fail to understand how painfully they must have acted upon those who first heard them.

Of the humanity of the Christ I have already spoken, and how that feeling of human kinship had appealed to the submerged masses of the old Roman Empire. The slave element played a much less prominent role in the Teutonic countries of the north. There were slaves and there were serfs and all kinds of people who belonged to those classes which were neither entirely free nor entirely slave. But in a purely agricultural community, where there were no very rich and no very poor, there was no such difference of position as in the commercial realm of ancient Rome, where one was either a millionaire or a hopeless pauper living in a squalid eighth-floor tenement on the outskirts of the city.

There was another appeal. I have already hinted at it, and I will now mention it in greater detail. The people of Germanic stock were accustomed to being ruled by one chief who invariably surrounded himself with a council of elders and who was maintained in his high office by the conviction of the other members of the tribe that he was best fitted for the job—that he was best fitted to lead them in battle and to govern them in times of peace. The new God of the Christians was in this respect very much like their old Wotan. He was indeed a mighty Lord, and the saints who surrounded Him were a fine council of elders. And then there was His Son, and that was a new motif within the realm of religion. For this Son had not been killed as other gods had been, but three days after His death He had been resurrected and after His return to life

Chapter IX

He had for quite a long time dwelt among His former friends so that they could convince themselves that He had indeed risen from the dead and that His promise that He would return had been no idle boast. And someday—and this was a terrific point in favor of those who told these multitudes about Him—He would actually return and would then sit in judgment on the living and the dead. We can no longer understand what it must have meant to these simple-minded people to know (not to guess or to suspect, but to *know*) that the Deputy of the All-Highest would at some definite date in the near future come back to this earth, that He would mount the high seat of judgment, would call for the roll containing the names of all those who had ever spent even a few hours on this earth, would carefully examine the evidence written against everybody's name, and thereupon would issue His decree that would either send a man to enjoy the everlasting bliss of heaven or condemn him to the eternal tortures of hell.

Hell no longer means very much to us. I realize, of course, that in saying this I speak for myself and for the sort of people with whom I have spent most of my days and that there are still millions who are firmly convinced that there is such a place and who think that Signor Dante wrote a pretty accurate guidebook of the infernal regions. But the unbelievers are now so greatly in the majority that the others form a divided minority and usually stick closely to their own kind without bothering the rest of us with a story that makes us smile quite as much as if they had expressed their belief in witches and witchcraft.

This may be one of the reasons we find it so difficult to understand the so-called Middle Ages. Then everybody (even that archheretic, the Emperor Frederick II, whose tomb was recently bombed by our army in Sicily) knew that those two localities called heaven and hell were realities. He was born on a small flat disk that floated in space, and above, hidden by the dome of the blue sky, there was a heaven where all was peace and happiness and contentment, where there were no poor and no rich, and where there was neither sickness nor death, but glory everlasting, amen. Way down below there was a deep dark pit where hideous devils with asbestos skins pranced around with long pitchforks to keep the tortured souls in the heat of those fires which scorched them without ever consuming their lacerated flesh.

How and from whom and from where the Christians had inherited hell is a fascinating story, but I have not got space to follow it in detail. Suffice it to say that hell existed just as Sing Sing prison exists, and though few of us have ever been in Ossining, we know that there is such a place as this dreadful living tomb and that, if we commit certain acts one should not commit, we will go there and will have to atone for our error in judgment. Of course, a modern criminal figures that perhaps he will be lucky and get away with his crime. But in A.D. 700 or 800 or even 900 there was no chance of his getting away with anything. For he would be brought not before a worldly court, where the judges might perhaps not be so bright and might overlook a few points and give the accused the benefit of the doubt, and where a slick lawyer might persuade the jury to disagree upon his guilt. But with the second coming of Christ (a possibility that was unquestioned by those people) all worldly courts of justice would come to an end. There would be a divine tribunal, presided over by one single magistrate—the omniscient Son of the true God—from Whom not a single scrap of evidence could possibly remain hidden. With this powerful spiritual weapon in their hands, those Christian missionaries who converted our ancestors to their faith had their parishioners completely at their mercy. A few rare souls would now and then be gained by the visions of God's love and mercy. The rest, being what they were, barbarians and semi-savages, had to be persuaded to behave themselves by arguments of a more practical sort, and hell was the most powerful of these.

Gradually, after the ominous year 1000 (when nothing of earthshaking consequence happened), the belief in the second coming of the Lord began to lose ground. Two hundred years later it had completely disappeared. Occasionally (even today) it might bob up in remote rural districts but would be discarded as idle newspaper talk or an outbreak of some obscure kind of insanity among sexually repressed people who are apt to fall victims to all kinds of queer manias. The belief in hell, however, maintained itself much longer, and it was an effective means by which to make the average citizen at least keep within certain bounds of decency. Especially at first the prospect of eternal torture had a most salutary influence upon all sorts of people who otherwise would have been infinitely worse than they now dared to be. They were often pretty bad in spite of all the threats of eternal punishment the Church held over their heads. But by and large there was an improvement. Mercy became a pleasant ingredient of everyday life, and the recipient of this unexpected blessing did not ask whether it was inspired by love or by fear. He knew that he was not going to be unjustly dragged to the gallows, that his wife and children were not going to be sold unjustly into slavery, and that his property was not going to be unjustly taken away from him. By the same token, the bully who always had everything his own way because he knew the fear in which he was held by his neighbors now came to hesitate before he landed his fist on the eye of a harmless fellow citizen, lest he should happen to be guilty of such an outrage on the Lord's day or during one of those periods which the Church had proclaimed as the Truce of God.

That the Church with particular vehemence suppressed all human sacrifice is a point I need not stress. Human sacrifice (which was to play such a hideous role in the lives of the Norse-

men who were wont, at the death of a chieftain, to send him
forth upon his last voyage surrounded by his slain servants) had
already begun to disappear from those parts of the world that
had been exposed to the beneficent rule of imperial Rome.
But with Christianity it became a sin so terrible that even in
the remote regions of this wilderness no heathenish priest any
longer dared to cut the throat of a human sacrificial victim.

And so, in every department of their daily lives, these recently baptized children of nature began to lose some of those
traces which only too strongly betrayed their animal origin.
This did not mean that they became totally civilized. Torture
was not yet abolished. Serfdom continued to exist. Unwanted
children were still turned into foundlings, but now such a fate
no longer meant death to the poor infants, as the Church took
them under its care, and pious sisters would devote themselves
to bringing them up in the path of righteousness and the fear
of the Lord.

And then—as the Church thought—there was a chance of
atoning for the evil we had done in this world by devoting
part (or all) of our worldly treasures to such good deeds as
the founding of hospitals, homes for the aged, and asylums for
the lepers, not to mention the building of still more churches
and monasteries. All of which was as much of a step forward
as the legislation by which the British government in India
put an end to the more disgusting manifestations of piety
among the teeming multitudes along the Ganges and the
Brahmaputra. The difference was that the poor Britishers had
to depend upon soldiers and policemen to enforce their rules,
which always gave a lot of sentimental folk a fine chance to
howl about "brutal oppression," whereas the Church could
achieve the same purpose by means of spiritual repression, in
which case nobody could object. And though I would hardly
claim that my ancestors of a thousand years ago had suddenly
become a group of gentle, law-abiding, or even righteous citi-

zens, I feel sure that they were an enormous improvement upon what they and their fathers and grandfathers had been before. They still had a very long way to travel before they began to show symptoms of being truly civilized, but now at least they had been shown the forward path, traveling on which would make them a little less like their remote predecessors of the cave and the stone ax who would cleave the skull of anyone not belonging to their own tribe.

And finally—and that is what I have had in mind all during this chapter—how did all this affect me, how am I today a product of what happened when the people of my native marshes were converted to Christianity? It would be very hard to say. I have never been a very good Christian in the accepted sense of the word, as I shall tell you afterwards. Yet I am conscious of certain traces of that primitive Christian faith in my own make-up, and I am sure that everybody is, including Comrade Stalin of the Kremlin, Moscow, and his playmates who not so very long ago decided to eradicate even the last vestiges of a faith that they called the spiritual opium of the poor.

The fear of hell which played such a decisive role in the lives of the people who lived between the tenth and the nineteenth centuries merely makes us smile. Neither can we find an attractive prospect in the vision of a heaven populated by the kind of people we never wanted to meet while we were on this earth. And we have accepted certain ethical standards which, so I hope, guide us in our dealings with our fellow men as infallibly as the hope of any kind of eternal reward. I realize, however, that in order to get that far we had to pass through different stages of development and that this primitive Christian experiment was the basis on which we had to construct what came afterwards.

Several times in my life I have been forced to face death. Those were among the most interesting moments of my entire career, for at such moments God calls one's bluff, if I may so express myself without giving offense to those of my neighbors who are not on such pleasantly intimate terms with the Almighty as I happen to be. For He does exist in my consciousness in a late medieval form—a kind and very wise old gentleman, a sort of beneficent grandfather with whom I occasionally hold conversation and discuss my own little problems. I have often asked Him to give me at least an inkling of what such minds as those of Charlemagne or Otto the Great were like —what those people of that hopelessly distant and incomprehensible age thought about the world in which they lived— what the figure of Christ really meant to them—what their attitude towards their womenfolk and their children was. For if I could really find this out, I should be the greatest historian who ever set pen to paper, and from my tenth year on (or even earlier) I wanted more than anything else to be a very famous historian.

But whenever I touched upon this subject, He would smile pleasantly. And the good father was right in the little story which you will find in my foreword: He has indeed the kindest and most pleasant smile ever seen in heaven or on earth. And He would say, "My child, I gave you a will of your own and a fairly good brain (though you might have made better use of it) that you should find these things out for yourself. If you knew all the answers, I myself should become superfluous, and I have no intention whatsoever of resigning, at least not for a good many eternities to come."

Which serves to explain my dive back into the slender literature that exists upon this age of anarchy and chaos, when every city—and therefore every archive—was sure to be burned down at least a couple of times every hundred years or so. Naturally, I shall therefore not try to throw any further light upon this dark subject, for my own little candle burns none too brightly when I descend into the vault that holds the mortal remains of these—to us—so hopelessly mysterious people. But I needed this rather elaborate description of my ancestors—some thirty generations removed—if I wanted to make clear to myself what the triumph of Christianity in our part of the world meant towards making us of today what we happen to be. I could have done much better if my ignorance upon the subject had not been quite so profound as it actually is. Maybe I will find out in another dozen years or so, but then, alas! it will be too late.

I Plan to Become a Feudal Knight but Discover That My Intentions Are Not So Well Understood as They Should Have Been

WHEN I was eleven years old (or was it ten?), I quite unexpectedly became a landowner—on a very small scale—but a landowner just the same.

A short time before we had moved from Rotterdam to The Hague and had acquired a garden—the first garden that ever entered into my life, for most of the houses in the ancient part of Rotterdam did not even boast of a back yard. I still remember the dimensions of our park. It was seven meters wide and thirty-five meters long—about twenty-three feet by one hundred and fourteen. At the far end, this side of the lane separating us from the Roman Catholic cemetery, where the nightingales sang so beautifully in the high old trees, I had my property. It was about twenty-three by fifteen feet, and one third of that space was taken up by a small wooden barn that one of our predecessors must have built as a tool shed or storeroom—I never knew which. Nor did it matter. I now had a piece of land of my own and a house of my own. When you are ten years old, this means a lot, for you will be envied by all the neighboring boys who do not have a piece of land and a house of their own, and none did.

Chapter X

At first it was suggested that I turn my land into a formal garden. A few clumps of grass had been left over after my parents had put their own demesne in order. These were arranged in circular form by the man who had undertaken to put in order the weedy wilderness the former tenant had left us, and I was supposed to spend twenty cents of my own money (and my weekly stipend was five cents Dutch) on flower seeds.

The idea did not appeal to me the least little bit. Fifty years ago, flower seed did not come as it does today in lovely little envelopes showing the finished product as being of such dimensions and such magnificent coloring that no child can withstand their appeal. When I was young, you went to a seed store and bought the queer-looking stuff (if I remember correctly, spinach was the queerest-looking of them all) at so much per gram, and the seed man, who was always slightly dusty and who wore steel-rimmed glasses, weighed it out on a pair of apothecary scales. The whole transaction was very prosaic and had none of the fascination that my grandchildren experience when they go to Lake's drugstore in Old Greenwich and stand entranced by the beautiful floral dream displayed on the seed counter, located between the cigars and cigarettes and the empty spot where there was, in prewar days, a rich assortment of imported French perfumes.

As I also knew that it would be a great many weeks before my seeds would begin to peep modestly from beneath their earthen blanket and had had very sad experiences with the beans I used to cultivate in my sponge box (I belong to the slate age, and was never entrusted with a piece of paper until I could really write), this idea of starting a regular flower garden did not appeal to me at all. One morning I got up very early and simply removed that charming grass pattern which the gardener had laid out on "my" land, and when the family arose, they had to accept a *fait accompli*. Their horticultural experiment had failed. I just had no talent or natural inclination for that sort of thing.

But they were hardly prepared for what I did next. The little wooden shed of which I spoke a moment ago had served as a hotel, a western blockhouse perpetually attacked by bands of wild Injuns, a general store, a railroad depot, and a Roman fortress besieged by our noble Batavian ancestors. But now it became something else—a medieval castle, and it became a medieval castle because I had read a book.

That book should have a chapter by itself, for it did more to shape my life during my early and most impressionable years than any other influence, including parents, home, and friends. I do not mention the church, although I realize that everybody who writes about his youth is at this moment supposed to tell how deeply he was impressed by his Bible and William Shakespeare. The immortal William was nothing but a name to me, and a very vague name, too. He existed in an excellent Dutch translation—the labor of love of a professional botanist who had devoted all his spare time to this Herculean task. He had done a most excellent job, and we had the whole collection in our small library, for it was supposed to add considerable luster to a respectable Dutch household to have the combined efforts of William Shakespeare and L. A. J. Burgersdijk on their shelves. I did not know who Master Shakespeare had been, but when I picked up one of the volumes (bearing the intriguing name of *Hamlet*), I noticed that it had something to do with history and therefore must be something up my own little alley. But the story was beyond me, and I could make nothing of the melancholy Dane. He seemed rather silly. Very full of words and terribly sorry for himself, but without any desire to do anything about his uncomfortable position.

I may not have thought it out that way when I was quite so young and this may be a judgment of my later days, for such things are very apt to get themselves rather badly mixed up.

Chapter X

I remember, however, for a certainty that my first encounter with the great bard was not a success. And, if I am to be entirely honest with myself, I never got over a certain feeling of boredom when exposed to the good William of the second-best bed, either in the printed form of the endless editions which since then have been bestowed upon me or as presented on the stage in beautiful costumes that go from Brooks (the theatrical outfitters, not the haberdashers on Madison Avenue) to the theatrical storehouse of the Messrs. Eaves.

If I had never read *Hamlet,* I should not know to this day whether Hamlet married his girl or not. For by the end of the twenty-seventh scene, I usually get so fidgety and my legs begin to shake so violently that the neighbors who are involuntarily being kicked in the posterior parts (you know how narrow our theater seats are) begin to object, and Jimmie takes me out to prevent a public scandal.

The other day I decided to try again, and, since I thought that my son and Gracie (both of whom are still very young) needed a little Shakespeare for their education, I took them along, though I had to bribe them by the promise of a luncheon at the St. Regis, which raised the ante to quite a considerable sum. It was a fine performance by a most dignified group of mummers. But after an hour or so I got a vicious kick on the shins, and Gracie hissed at me that my snoring interfered considerably with the pleasure of the other spectators who had also paid $2.75 for the privilege of hearing the Danish prince recite his little piece about to be or not to be, and that unless I could keep awake she and Willem had better take me out and walk me around the block until I regained consciousness.

Outside in the lobby I asked them, "Well, do you like it?" They said no. It had bored them to extinction, and they never would have come if I had not insisted on it. Whereupon we went to the Algonquin and had tea and talked to Frank Case, who told us that since all the Hamlets of the last half century had been his patrons, he had felt duty-bound to go and see their performances. "But did you like them?" we inquired.

"Oh, well," said tactful Frank, "it is hardly up to me to say anything against a fellow author." And there the matter was dropped.

Shakespeare, therefore, is out as one of the great literary influences upon my youth, and I am sorry to say that the same thing holds good for the Bible. My parents and practically all my relatives and their friends had long since broken with the church. If sometimes they were reproached for this attitude of an almost complete indifference towards every established form of religion, they would answer that it was not they who had left the church but that it was the church which had deserted them. That answer meant nothing to me then, but I now understand what they meant. The liberalism of the eighteenth century (what the pious folk denounced as the "wicked Voltairianism") had politely (and sometimes not quite so politely) rejected every kind of dogma. The person of Jesus had been retained, but merely as a great ethical teacher without any supernatural qualifications. He was different from the other Jewish messiahs because he preached love rather than indignation, but the idea of his having been the Son of God was rejected as a fairy story, on a par with the full-panoplied Minerva who had jumped forth from the head of Zeus.

This was not meant in a sacrilegious way. Not in the least. The weakening of the strictly religious feelings among the better-educated classes had run parallel to a tremendous increase in what, for lack of a better word, we might call their ethical consciousness. During the latter half of the eighteenth century they were no longer content with the pleasant platitude that the poor were no doubt somewhat of a nuisance but could be dismissed from the mind if we took the necessary steps to prevent them from starving to death.

But during the second half of the eighteenth century a few

enlightened people had begun to ask the uncomfortable question: "Why should the poor always be with us?" and they had hit upon the same answer we ourselves have found—their ignorance and intellectual backwardness had kept them in a state of bondage, and education was the answer to the dreadful problem of poverty. And everywhere there had been a stirring of the mind until a veritable crusade of enlightenment had swept across the country.

Perhaps the expression "swept" is a little too strong, for the Hollander of the eighteenth century had been much too comfortable and much too leisurely ever to let himself be "swept" into anything. But under the leadership of a kindhearted and liberal-minded Baptist minister, one Maarten Nieuwenhuizen, a society had been formed which bore the dignified title of the Society for the Benefit of the Community at Large, a sort of mixture of our modern Unitarianism and Ethical Culture. The prospectus with which this Monnickendam dominie had started his movement had very definitely explained the purpose of the organization, which by means of lectures and public gatherings and the publication of a simple kind of literature did not intend merely to improve the mind of the better situated classes—it also hoped to appeal to the "common man," that even the poor might be benefited by an increased familiarity with all the greatest products of art and literature and with the social developments of the last fifty years. When this program proved an instant success (it was the year 1784, and for the last twenty years everybody had been reading Jean-Jacques Rousseau's *Emile* and discussing that famous man's pedagogical ideals), the society had extended its labors into the field of education and had begun a bold campaign for a better system of schools for the poor and underprivileged.

When I was young, that organization still flourished, and one of my earliest recollections is of being taken to the lectures (with lantern slides) of the Nut, as the society was gen-

erally known. This name, inscribed on the schools the organization still maintains in many small cities—the Nut School—
never fails to cause great merriment among visiting Americans.
But the Dutch word *nut* (like the German *nützen*) is related
to our own *need* or *benefit,* and those schools played a very important role in the intellectual development of the Netherlands of the last hundred and fifty years. For although Nieuwenhuizen had been exposed to the most violent opposition
on the part of the established church, which had denounced
him, as, a few years later, President Timothy Dwight of Yale
was to denounce Thomas Jefferson, as a "wild beast," he had
met with such widespread sympathy for his ideas that his
cultural and social conception had become the accepted religion of the class of Dutch to which my own family happened
to belong. They were good Christians during six days of the
week, but bad churchgoers on Sunday, and that, of course,
made them an easy target for the followers of the old orthodoxy who never tired of depicting them as godless heathen,
worshipers of Baal and enemies of society.

It was the old, old story. Indeed, the skeptic who coined the
terrible phrase that all slavery is self-imposed may well have
been right. For these ethical brethren and sisters were working
day and night to improve the fate of their less fortunate neighbors and to set them free from the yoke imposed upon them
by the Calvinistic theocracy which ruled them with the iron
rod of their Old Testament Jehovah. But these poor creatures
as a rule rejected every effort to help them and cherished their
abject position in society with a sort of sadistic pleasure in their
own misery.

This in turn was resented by their self-appointed saviors,
and in the end the church and the liberals completely parted
company. At court there was still an outward tendency towards
the observation of a strict orthodoxy, which was perhaps just
as well, as His Majesty King Willem III, during whose benevo-

lent rule I had the honor to be born, would hardly have quali-
fied as a member of any kind of "cultural society," and those
who aspired to be considered eligible for courtly honors would
also patronize the regular Sunday-morning services. But it
must have been a very uncomfortable experience for them.
They filled their pews with the beautiful green cushions (often
modestly embroidered with their coats of arms) and they
opened their ancestral Bibles with the heavy brown leather
bindings and the resplendent brass locks, and they dutifully
read the text announced for the day's sermon, but when they
finally lifted their eyes to examine their surroundings, they
beheld a vast vacuum—that space which under normal circumstances should have been occupied by the "better middle
classes" who at that very moment were taking their children
for a walk through God's green nature, there to teach them
the glories of creation by making them familiar with the beauties of the fields and the birds of the air and the little fishes
that disported themselves in the waters beneath the sky.

It is true that the uncomfortable benches in the back of the
church were all occupied. But there the "common people"
were herded together—those too poor to pay for the privilege
of a regular private seat. And even though it must have flattered the pride of the ladies and gentlemen in their private
pews to leave the House of Prayer between the serried ranks of
the "gray ones," as the nondescript, evil-smelling, badly clad
masses of the common people had been called for untold centuries, with their caps dutifully pulled from their none too
clean scalps, they cannot have failed to feel profoundly in-
censed at the idea that of the really "nice" people (their doctors
and lawyers and the better class of merchants and shopkeepers),
scarcely one found his way to the official place of worship.

Out of this situation had grown a sort of triumvirate, composed of the old, orthodox clergy, the older ruling classes (who
even after the present war for democracy may make a bid for

the rulership), and the lowest orders of society. On occasions this proved a very handy arrangement. The reverend gentlemen kept the mob under control and the Best Families, by means of their prestige among the men of God, could turn the wrath of the disinherited masses against anybody who had incurred their displeasure.

Of course, this power had to be used very carefully. The days were gone when a mob of the lowest dregs of society could be allowed to murder the greatest Dutch statesman of the seventeenth century, Jan De Witt, and when a court of justice could be packed with tools willing to send the liberal-minded John of Barneveldt (in many ways, the Thomas Jefferson of the Dutch Republic) to the scaffold. But if handled deftly and circumspectly, this Greek chorus of the underfed could still be used to make its appearance at the appropriate moment, and everybody knew it and kept this threat firmly in mind, most of all the liberals, who repaid the clergy with a neglect and a contempt that made itself evident upon every possible occasion.

Until my twelfth or fourteenth year I never met a single person who ever went to church, who had been confirmed, or who had been married or intended to be buried by a minister of the official church. Needless to say, under those circumstances I was not brought into contact with the Bible, either as literature or as the fountainhead of all worldly and heavenly wisdom. What I knew about the Christian religion I got from those allusions to Holy Writ which had incorporated themselves into the vernacular (and the Dutch language is brimful of them) and from those concrete remnants of the old Catholic faith which were all around me in the shape of ancient churches, street names, and the festive days of the year, such as Christmas and Easter and Whitsuntide, which of course we observed because they were public holidays.

I remember that on one occasion, while rummaging through

Chapter X

our small library, I came upon a book entitled *Biblical Stories Retold for the Benefit of the Christian Youth*. It was quite an old edition in a dark yellow cover, and it was beautifully illustrated with all the more gruesome episodes of the Old Testament. Most of them delighted my heart, for every child loves scenes of bloodshed and torture. But one page frightened me greatly. It showed a great many children being devoured by bears, while a bald-headed gentleman in some kind of Oriental garb stood by, wildly waving his arms in encouragement of the ferocious monsters who were making a meal of the little boys and girls. The text informed me that the bald-headed old gentleman was the prophet Elisha (an otherwise kindhearted person who had spent all his days raising widows' sons from death, feeding a hundred soldiers with only twenty loaves of bread, and making iron float on the water). He had become so exasperated at the taunts of a gang of forty-two youngsters (the exact number of the victims was duly given) who had derided him for his lack of hirsute adornment that he had cursed them and had called forth two she-bears who had torn the children to pieces.

This struck me as a most uncharitable act and certainly unworthy of a man who pretended to speak with the voice of God. If one were bald, that too must have been an act of God, and why get so terribly angry at anybody who drew attention to the fact? My own grandfather too was bald, and my aunts were forever encouraging me to pull his wig off (for which act I was afterwards rewarded with an extra supply of cookies), but he had never produced any she-bears to tear me to pieces. At the very worst he had boxed my ears, but as a rule he had said, "Children will be children," and had let it go at that. Why this horrible carnage of forty-two (count them—forty-two!) little Jewish children who had done nothing worse than what I myself was always being told to do and which brought me an extra dividend in sweets? And during the night after I had read this chapter in the *Biblical Stories Retold for the Benefit of the Christian Youth* I had such a terrible nightmare that my shrieks hastily brought my parents to my bedside.

"Oh, Mummy," I cried, "those terrible bears will eat me up! I pulled Opa's wig off this afternoon and showed his bald head, and now those two horrible bears will eat me up!"

I was of course duly consoled and told that it was a foolish story in a foolish book, but when next day I wanted to go back to my Biblical literature, the book was gone, and I never saw it again.

That was my first and last encounter with the Old Testament during the first dozen years of my life, and it would therefore be foolish to pretend that the Bible played any kind of role during my so-called "formative years." But this does not mean that I remained untouched by any kind of literary influence while I was still at that age when a child's soul is like a clean slate upon which the goddess of chance may engrave almost any kind of message.

All of us have had one particular book which in some queer way has influenced the rest of our days. Some of us have actually forgotten what that book was. Others have done so deliberately, feeling slightly ashamed that such a piece of literary claptrap (as we afterwards discovered it to be) could once upon a time have meant so much to us that it set a definite stamp upon all our subsequent acts. Yes, even long after we recognized the utter literary worthlessness of our best-beloved bedtime story, we lived under its spell and were, to a certain extent, guided by its moral and worldly lessons.

I found that never-to-be-forgotten volume almost thirty years after I had lost sight of it. It belonged to one of my nieces, and she let me have it. I took my treasure home and wondered what horrible disappointment awaited me, but it was not so bad as I had expected. It was a serial story which had appeared in a Dutch monthly that had been the equivalent of the Amer-

ican *St. Nicholas Magazine* of half a century ago. It was edited
by an honorable schoolmaster who lived remotely in a small
village in the province of Zeeland. He was a good and worthy
man, but his budget was apparently very limited, and as a result he was obliged to use whatever illustrations he could get by
buying the cuts from French and English and German publishers. I know that now because I have for many years been in
the business myself. At the time that the arrival of every new
issue of my beloved magazine meant a day of joy and surrepti-
tious reading late into the night, I merely noticed that the illustrations did not always cover the story as it was told in the
text, but sometimes wandered considerably from the subject
and were therefore a bit perplexing, for one was likely to find
palm trees growing in what was supposed to be a Dutch
meadow, and reindeer made their appearance among the Swiss
Alps. But why be fussy? The story was the thing, and what a
story!

The hero was a minstrel of the early part of the thirteenth
century. As behooved a true son of the Middle Ages, he was devoted heart and soul to the cause of his master, and his master
was none but that sadly misguided Count Willem II of Holland who felt it his duty to make a bid for the crown of the Holy
Roman Empire. I can understand why he felt that way. Most
historians have either overlooked him completely or have dismissed him as an overambitious young man who should have
let well enough alone. But he belonged to a family which had
now ruled the county of Holland for almost three consecutive
centuries (quite a record in those days) and which was related
to all the more successful dynasties of that day.

Anyone who has ever been in The Hague (before the Nazis
ruined the heart of that lovely city) and who has seen the Hall
of the Knights there will realize that the counts of Holland of
the thirteenth century were people of considerable importance.
Only very rich people could ever have afforded to build them-

selves a palace as imposing as the old Ridderzaal. And it must have taken more than a well-filled treasury to erect so stately a hall in what was still a very remote part of the civilized half of Europe. Willem II it was who decided to pull down the old wooden hunting lodge on the site and to replace it by a stone structure that would show his haughty neighbors of Flanders and Burgundy that he too was able to do something in the architectural line of which even the King of France might have been proud. He did not live to see the finished product, for he was killed most ignominiously in a row with some rebellious peasants from western Frisia. But it was quite natural that a young man of his ambitions and his extraordinary qualities should have thought of running for the emperorship of that Holy Roman Empire of which the late Lord Bryce so rightly said that it was not holy or Roman or an empire. But during the middle of the thirteenth century it was about the best thing Europe had to offer in the way of elective offices. It was not an easy job to get. It took a lot of practical electioneering, wire-pulling, and plain and indirect bribery to obtain a sufficient number of votes in the electoral college, and only candidates with the best kind of social references and ability to draw large bills of exchange upon the moneylenders had a chance of getting to first base.

In order to build up as reliable an organization as he could get, this bright young ruler had gone democratic and had associated himself with the cities along the Rhine, which were experiencing their first boom since the days of the Romans and were delighted to have a real prince to represent their interests.

That was the background against which my minstrel performed his valorous deeds. He was the intelligence officer of the young Count. He went from town to town and from castle to castle, disguised as a simple minstrel, but in reality plotting and scheming to bring about the election of his lord and master as head of the Holy Roman Empire.

Chapter X

This historical part was still very hazy to me, but I was completely fascinated by the mighty deeds which my beloved jon-
gleur performed on almost every page of our monthly install-
ments. No situation could be too tough for him. No plot on the
part of his enemies was ever able to envelop him in its snares.
Being obliged to travel in the disguise of an itinerant fiddler,
he could not carry arms, but his favorite weapon was an iron
stave which looked like a plain walking stick and which was so
heavy that no one but himself could wield it. With this he
knocked a knight down from his horse as if he had been a child
riding a cockhorse. And in case of need, whole rows of knights
went that way. Furthermore, he was a most marvelous athlete,
to whom it meant nothing to outrun a horse, while sleep and
rest were little items he could disregard with supreme disdain.
Even sickness played practically no role in his life, for when an
enemy got him contaminated with leprosy (sending a note to
him by means of a leprous messenger), he immediately had the
address of a friendly witch who by means of herbs and salves
cured him in no time at all.

But the field in which he most distinguished himself was that
of music. He was fairly well versed in the art of painting, but
painting had not yet come into its own (another century and a
half had to go by before the brothers van Eyck were to ply
their trade at the Castle in the Woods, which is what 's Graven-
hage—"the Hedge of the Counts"—means), and so he specialized
in singing, fiddling, and improvising. But as a trouvère (someone who made up his verses as he went along), a fiddler, and
a harpist he stood supreme.

As I told you, some thirty years later I found a bound volume
of this monthly among the books of one of my nieces, and I
appropriated it in return for some other and more modern
books she desired. I took my treasure home and read it or
rather tried to read it, as it had no literary value whatsoever
and merely consisted of a number of incidents very badly

strung together and without any sense of sequence. The wooden figures moved clumsily across the stage and, as for my hero, he resembled the *Faust* of a small French provincial town, done according to the best traditions of Monsieur Charles Gounod, the distinguished Parisian composer who was so successful in bringing the works of Johann Sebastian Bach to the attention of the general public by providing the first piece of Herr Bach's *Well-Tempered Clavichord* with a charming little obbligato of his own.

But at the age of twelve one does not care much about literary values. The story is the thing, and that story, preposterous as it was, made more impression upon me than anything I have read since those happy days when every month was filled with eager anticipation about what the great man was going to do next. On the whole, I am grateful that I made his acquaintance, for, clumsily though he was drawn, he had a streak of genuine nobility in him. That word "nobility" has not fared very well these last thirty years. Our democratic age is apt to associate it with aristocracy, and whenever it is mentioned people unconsciously think of those brilliant young men of Italian, Polish, or French origin who, as Count Ugibugi or Prince Sladeropski or the Marquis Pré Salé, grace the society columns of our newspapers, most of them being unmitigated heels who should never have seen the western exposure of the Statue of Liberty. But they have no more to do with the real meaning of the word "nobility" than the qualification of best-seller has to do with the literary value of a book that is being forced upon the public as the latest manifestation of our native genius.

I have always explained the word to my own children by adding a *k* to it. Then they would understand its meaning as something that is so outstanding that it deserves to be "known" by all the world for its perfection. And I believe (though I am not a very good philologist) that it is all mixed up with the Greek root *gno,* which spooks around in all the Greek words which have to do with knowledge, discovery, and understanding and with the Latin *gnoscere* and *noscere,* which meant "to acquire knowledge." That is how I like to explain my own affection for the good old expression that something is endowed with a quality of nobility because it deserves to be "known" by all men.

My absurd hero, with all his literary shortcomings, richly deserved to be known, at least by all little boys, for he never did a mean thing, and he had to work hard for everything he got. And if sometimes he committed deeds of such preposterous valor that my uncles and aunts whom I asked to read his story to me smiled at me with good-natured indulgence, it certainly did me no harm at that particular stage of my career to be exposed to an influence which inspired me to acts of unselfish loyalty and devotion, no matter how sadly I have fallen short of those ideals in later life. And the story had another great advantage over most juvenile books of today. It was sentimental, but it never turned maudlin. The weeping Magdalen, with her swollen red eyes, who bestowed that unfortunate expression upon our long-suffering language, never intruded herself into the proceedings, and as a matter of fact, like Howard Pyle's *Men of Iron,* which was written at about the same time, the book did not greatly bother about women. They were there, but they remained in the background, tending to the business of the knights' hall, the refectory, the servants' quarters, the weaving looms, and the nursery. On occasion they could receive treatment as rough as that meted out to the heroine of Voltaire's *Candide,* but they bore up remarkably well under their harrowing experiences. And somehow or other the author (whose name I don't know to this day) had caught the spirit of the thirteenth century, when, under the influence of Provence, the only remaining civilized part of medieval Europe, women ceased to be the household chattels they had been with the barbarians who had over-thrown the old world and became an object of worship and veneration.

This too had its influence upon me. I liked to imagine my-self in the role of a page at the court of some Queen Jehanne or Eleanore of Les Baux, though I am sorry to say that when-ever I played this role I was at once suspected of having com-mitted some hidden sin and of now trying to gain favor by an exhibition of manners which were not at all in keeping with my usual behavior.

Such first imprints, however, upon a child's character can never be entirely wiped out. That slightly quixotic approach towards women always stuck to me and probably accounted for my failures in dealing with the gentler sex (God save the mark!) during the rest of my life. I never quite got over the feeling that all women lived on a sort of pedestal (some of course a little higher and some a little lower) and longed to be the heroines of one of those romantic episodes which were common incidents in the lives of the medieval troubadours. It was only a great many years later and at cost of terrific wear and tear upon my emotions and upon my bank account that I learned that the troubadour business had indeed gone out with Guiraut Riquier (who died in the year 1294) and that all efforts made since then to revive the era of the chivalresque approach had been lamentable failures. I realize, of course, that Hollywood has since then come to our rescue by giving us certain new ideas of romance, based upon the standards prevailing in the City of the Angels. I have studied them most carefully, as they are part of the general pattern of our modern culture, but I grieve to say that, in spite of many unhappy personal experiences, I still cling to the ideals of the thirteenth century. This may reveal an unsuspected conservative streak in my make-up. To which I can only answer that such a streak of conservatism is undoubtedly present, but it is too late now

I wanted to be a young minstrel entertaining the noble folk at a castle.

Instead of being a handsome young minstrel, I was a com-
monplace little boy in a sailor suit, spending my evenings
doing Latin and Greek exercises.

to do anything about it. And of course when I was twelve years old, my attitude towards women was not really of very great importance.

On the other hand, the appeal of this book to my ambition was something that influenced my life for at least half a dozen years, and the years between twelve and eighteen count as much as those between the ages of one and four. I made, of course, a profound secret of my feelings about this story, for I knew by experience that whenever I got too much interested in a book it was likely to be taken away from me because it was suspected that it might interfere with my regular schoolwork, and in the Holland of half a century ago the school was a sacred institution, and nothing must interfere with the smooth functioning of the daily curriculum.

I therefore never let on to my decision to turn myself into an exact counterpart and replica of my beloved troubadour. Every morning and every evening I used to go through violent calisthenic exercises with a chair, for I had nothing else until I was fourteen years old, when I asked for a pair of dumbbells for my birthday, and got them too, though nobody quite understood what I wanted to do with them, as I was notorious for my indifferent behavior at the regular exercises in the school gymnasiums. These bored me, and unfortunately I had already got into the habit of not taking the slightest interest in whatever filled my young soul with weariness. Why should I suddenly want to become a Sandow? I knew that they would never understand if I told them, and so I pretended that I was privately trying to make up for my deficiencies at school. There was, of course, very little opportunity for valorous deeds, but I had discovered a small window in the attic through which I could get out on the roof. Whenever I felt that nobody would surprise me, I climbed all the roofs of our own street. Why I never broke my neck is still a mystery to me. I had plenty of opportunity, for I used to walk upright in the zinc gutters (to have held on to the tiles would have been a sign of weakness), and those gutters, for at least half the year, were filled with either snow or wet leaves.

One defect in my heroic build-up received a great deal of attention. I have already explained that because of a foolish nursemaid I was desperately afraid of the dark. I tried to overcome this "terror by night," as the Good Book calls it, by forcing myself to go to the attic long after everybody else was asleep. I experienced all the horrors of which the twelve-year-old imagination was capable, but I never succeeded in curing myself of this deplorable affliction. Many years later, in Cornell, the shortest route from my room to downtown led through the cemetery, and it was a well-lit cemetery, but I had to force myself to take that road. Even today, darkness does things to me which I can in no way explain except as a survival of that state of panic into which I was thrown by that dumb nurse and her stories about the spook in the mirror.

Under normal circumstances, this overpowering ambition should have forced me to do well at school and to leave all other boys behind me in my studies, but it did not work out that way. Our teaching was completely uninspired, and I despised my fellow scholars, who sat there like little automata, their brains patiently lapping up whatever their teachers put before them. I felt convinced that I could do much better if I were only left to my own devices. Had my beloved minstrel gone to a nice private school to accumulate that vast store of heterogeneous information which allowed him to converse on equal terms with all the most learned men of his time? He had not. He had done it by himself, and why shouldn't I be able to do likewise? But as I had nobody to guide me in my reading, as public libraries were unknown (except the Royal Library, which did not admit little boys), and as the lending libraries charged five cents per week (and my total income was only ten cents), my intellectual diet was not exactly a balanced one and was apt to give me very uncomfortable attacks of indigestion.

Within certain fields, such as history and literature (Dutch literature, of course, for, although I knew a little French and German, the English language was still a completely closed book to me), I was way ahead of the other boys and got nothing but A's. Geography, too, found favor in my eyes, and I was (believe it or not) already experimenting with those animated maps which afterwards were to give a somewhat different flavor to my history and geography books. But I remained so completely cold to the appeals of my teacher of mathematics, that not once in my life could I do such a simple sum as $317 + 2458$ and make it come out more or less correctly.

And so, from a strictly pedagogical point of view, my minstrel did me very little good. He inspired me to strive after a great many things which lay entirely beyond my undeveloped intellectual powers. He made me scratch my way through the Beethoven Violin Concerto at a time when even Haydn's simplest sonatas were beyond my reach. And instead of letting me spend my Wednesday and Saturday half holidays playing football with the other boys, he sent me forth upon long solitary walks through the dunes or along the endless roads of our polders, where I felt his companionship and listened to his wise counsel, which unfortunately was my own counsel, since I had nobody else with whom to discuss those matters which were really uppermost in my mind but which would have been completely destroyed the moment I had exposed them to the realities of my everyday existence. And when, month after month, I came home with the most disappointing report cards, graced with A's for history and language and E's for everything else, it was really his fault that I did not do any better.

Yet I would not have missed him for anything in this world. For he took me, who otherwise might have been hopelessly lost on the sea of commonplace self-contentment (and the Holland of half a century ago was just that), and gave me a purpose in life.

I had been brought up without any particular religious interests. The prevailing philosophical ideas were way beyond the understanding of a child. I needed a definite ideal after which to pattern my own life, and I found that ideal in this medieval minstrel. Looking at him from my present sophisticated point of view, I realize that he was an entirely preposterous figure, resembling one of those paper dolls which children cut out of their magazines and then dress up like a king or a knight or a common soldier. I have never even tried to translate his story for the benefit of either my children or my grandchildren, for they would never understand what it was all about. The whole setup is too hopelessly dated. And with me the generation that may perhaps remember this yarn will disappear and die out. But to me, the old juggler and fiddler and fighter meant the greatest influence in my life, for he took me into that realm of the imagination where I have lived ever since.

It was only natural that, being in this pleasant way introduced to the Middle Ages, I should want to know a lot more about that period, but I had a hard time getting at the necessary sources, for there were only a few history books in our library at home. However, I got hold of one of my father's school books and though it was as dull as the only Sunday-school sermon I ever heard (I was staying with a friend who attended these sacred doings), I dutifully read every word that had to do with the period from the tenth to the fifteenth centuries. In that way I learned of the existence, once upon a time, of an institution known as feudalism.

Chapter X

I should remark here that feudalism as an institution had never really prospered in the Low Countries by the North Sea, and it was only by a sort of break that they escaped its worst features. It is only very recently, and then under the guidance of two very lucid French historians, that I have really come to understand that strange social development of the early Middle Ages which so greatly influenced the lives of practically all other Europeans.

What really was feudalism? As every historian who has ever come in contact with the subject will tell you, it presents one of the simplest but at the same time one of the most complicated problems of the last five thousand years. And if there were any written evidence, he feels certain that he could trace it back to the very beginning of the human race. For feudalism is not something a bright, philosophically minded historian invented in the quiet seclusion of his ivory tower and then had accepted by a sufficient number of his neighbors to have it put to a practical test. It is as normal and unavoidable a result of certain specific social developments as cholera is the product of certain specific and unfortunate hygienic conditions. Get enough dirt and hunger and enough people with a low power of resistance together in any given spot and, the next thing you know, you will have a fine outbreak of a cholera epidemic on your hands; and let public safety and security descend to the point where it has practically disappeared, and, without anybody being conscious of what is actually happening, society (or what there is left of it) will congeal into solid bits of feudalism. The knight on horseback will make his appearance; the strong stone castle will arise from the top of the most nearly inaccessible hill; and huts with thatched roofs will begin to group themselves around the base of His Lordship's rock. For that knight on horseback and that castle on the rock represent the idea of safety to the barefooted peasants of the thatch-roofed cottages in the valley—and safety is the basic law of existence. Indeed, not even the humblest blades of grass can hope to survive without a certain degree of safety, and the same goes for the classes that live in the mud of Greenwich Cove and for the whales who disport themselves in the seas of the Antarctic.

It is all very well to talk of art and science and social justice and the Four or Five or Six Freedoms (they vary from time to time) as the desirable goals of life, but none of these will ever be able to develop unless their roots are firmly based in the soil of security. Security, therefore, is the beginning and end of our human civilization, but there can be no security without law. And law is but an empty word, written on a little piece of paper, without a policeman to see that it be enforced.

I have lived through a great many revolutions. These revolutions (like all revolutions since the beginning of time) only became possible the moment the policeman (and the soldiers acting as policemen) made common cause with the people. Before that stage had been reached, no outbreak of discontent ever had even the most remote chance of success. The policeman (and the soldier who is expected to help him out) must have reached the point where he has begun to feel a sense of absolute solidarity with the people, but when that final point of exasperation has been reached, there is no government on earth that can hope to survive.

Of course, what happens immediately afterwards is sometimes very unpleasant to those who have always lived under a system of law and order. That, however, cannot be helped. The actual process of birth is likely to be painful and uncomfortable to the patient, whether it be the birth of a child or of a new social and economic order of things—as we ourselves ought to know better than any other generation, since we are living in the midst of the greatest revolution of all times. The very discomfort of our daily existence ought to make us see it, although we are of course handicapped by the efforts of those who are interested in perpetuating the old order to make us believe that soon everything will be as it has always been, with two cars in every garage and a chicken in every pot. Two chickens in every garage and a handful of dried beans in every pot is much more likely to be the fate that awaits us during the next fifty years, but there is a general conspiracy of unconscious deceit on the part of those who are in charge of our economic destinies, and far be it from me to try and enlighten the public at large upon this point. I should accomplish less than nothing. I should be called a Bolshevik for my efforts, and my own source of revenue would be dried up.

All the same, I feel that I am right, for I have history on my side, and history is the most relentless of all witnesses. Well, then, history shows that, since there can be no survival without security (and survival is the basic law of existence), society must create conditions of security before it does anything else. That is why feudalism came into existence. Nobody had thought it out as a method of living. No social philosophers had burned the midnight oil (as they were to do so often afterwards and as they are doing twenty-four hours per day in our own age) to work out a new scheme that should bring about the Kingdom of Heaven on earth and that so often has succeeded in accomplishing the exact opposite. It just grew and developed because it was absolutely unavoidable if the human race was to survive. The Roman policeman, who for some four hundred years had patrolled every bailiwick from the Mediterranean to the North Sea, had left his beat, and nobody could locate him. He had definitely disappeared from the picture. For a while there was a hope that his place would be taken by the gendarmes of the great Frankish King, Carolus Magnus, who together with the Pope re-established some kind of Roman Empire upon a Teutonic rather than an Italian basis. But the Carolingian House was an ill-fated one. The Emperor's sons were sadly lacking in that force of character which had been the source of his strength and the cause of the respect in which he was held by the barbarians of the North.

Several years before the war, a learned German wrote an amusing book on the influence of accidents upon history. He was probably inspired by Pascal's famous dictum that if the nose of Cleopatra had been the twelfth of an inch longer or shorter, the whole subsequent history of the human race might have been different (neither Caesar nor Antonius might have fallen for her charm, while Augustus might have gone crazy about her), but he went much further than the great French mathematician, and the results of his investigations were positively startling. The temptation is great to reveal some of his secrets, but I mustn't, for otherwise this book would grow as long as the literary product of the late Joseph Smith, the inventor of Mormonism, though it would be a great deal more amusing. But few "accidents"—few "unpredictable incidents" —have played greater havoc with the normal development of history than the unexpected and high mortality rate among the dynasties who under happier circumstances might have become the established rulers of the greater part of central Europe.

We no longer bother about the principle of legitimacy. Our age, which is devoted to the worship of the common man (the basis of our modern kind of democracy), ridicules (if it does not actually distrust and despise) the idea that one family should be allowed to hold the job of chief executive for more than a few years at a time. After all, these Hapsburgs and Bourbons and Hohenzollerns and Orleanses and Bernadottes and Schleswig-Holsteins, and Oranges, to name only a few which still exist and function in whole and half-time jobs, what have they got that the Joneses and the Whites and the Smiths and the Williamses have not got? They are neither more beautiful (God knows they are not!) nor more brilliant than the plain people we send nowadays to the simple structures in which we house those we have elected to the temporary job of acting as our rulers. Except, of course, the shrewd Swiss, who have done away with even a semblance of one-man rule by giving the highest power in the state to a board of selectmen.

We wonder why people were for so many thousands of years quite so foolish as to accept and obey and revere these "anointed dynasties" when they knew perfectly well that the founders of these so-called "reigning families" may well have been swineherds or small Swiss farmers or clever gangsters or French innkeepers or cooks or ladies who had worked at a profession that may be very old but still has yet to be considered honorable. If we then read that many of the best brains of former times and men of the highest integrity were willing to sacrifice their lives and all their worldly possessions for them, we are completely lost and dismiss them as people who must have had a queer kink in their make-up, just like some of the religious fanatics we have known who seemed normal up to a certain point but who beyond that point went completely haywire and lost all contact with the realities of life. But if we should take the trouble to study the character of those persons, we would discover that the great majority of them were people of outstanding abilities—great scholars, the leading scientists of their day and age, men and women about whose intellectual and moral qualifications no one has ever felt the slightest trace of any kind of doubt. A few of them were conservatives or reactionaries because they had been born as such. A great many more were quite as liberal in most of their views as you and I, or more so; yet they had been out-and-out supporters of the monarchical ideal of government. And as I used to tell my students in the long-ago days when I was supposed to teach them the history of civilization: "Don't be too hasty in your judgment of a painting or a piece of music that is a recognized classic but that fails to please your own taste."

As a rule, when a picture or a symphony has for centuries enjoyed the approbation of those best fit to judge of its merits, it is likely to have qualities of lasting merit. But this does not hold good in all cases, for no rule connected with human emotions will hold good in all cases.